A. KOVALYOV

KV-028-749

MOSCOW

A SHORT GUIDE

FOREIGN LANGUAGES PUBLISHING HOUSE Moscow

А. Ковалев

ПО МОСКВЕ
Краткий путеводитель

CONTENTS

INTRODUCTION

Moscow is the capital of the U.S.S.R., the main city of the Russian Soviet Federal Socialist Republic (R.S.F.S.R.), and the centre of Moscow Region. It lies in the heart of the Russian Plain, between the rivers Oka and Volga, and is cut by the Moskva River and its major tributary, the Yauza. Several minor tributaries have been enclosed in underground canals and pipes.

The Moskva has its source in Moscow Region. It is 502 kilometres (312 miles) long and drains into the Oka near the town of Kolomna. Within city limits the river describes a number of curves over a stretch of more than 45 kilometres (28 miles), dividing the city into two unequal parts. The larger part, and the Kremlin, are on its high left bank, and the smaller, known as Zamoskvorechye, on the low right bank. Its width varies from 100 metres (328 feet) to 500 metres (1,640 feet) in the South Port area.

Moscow's *relief* is hilly, its south-western district on the Lenin Hills being more than 200 metres (656 feet) above sea-level. The *climate* is of the mild continental type, the winter usually lasting from mid-November to the end of March. The weather in winter is cloudy or overcast with abundant snowfalls. The average temperature (Centigrade) in January, the coldest month, is 11° below zero, and in particularly severe winters sometimes drops to 40° below zero. The mild summer lasts three months (June-August), the average temperature in July, the warmest month, being 20°. There are years, however, when it rises to 37° in the shade.

Administratively, the city, covering an area of 330 sq. kilometres (127.4 sq. miles) (figure of 1953), is divided into 25 districts with a total population, in early 1956, of 4,839,000 (excluding the suburbs).

The city is under the over-all administration of the Moscow City Soviet of Working People's Deputies, elected by the entire adult population of Moscow for every two years, and of its Executive Committee, comprising the Chairman, nine Deputy Chairmen, a Secretary and 14 Members. The present, sixth, Moscow City Soviet (elected in 1957) consists of 853 Deputies. The immediate administration of the various districts is in the hands of District Soviets of Working People's Deputies.

Moscow's 1957 budget totalled 6,755,053 thousand rubles, and expenditures 6,054,949 thousand rubles.

* * *

Moscow is the political, industrial, scientific and cultural centre of the country. It is the seat of the Government of the U.S.S.R., and of the Central Committee of the Communist Party of the Soviet Union. Sessions of the Supreme Soviet of the U.S.S.R., attended by Deputies from all ends of the country, are held in Moscow.

Thousands upon thousands visit the capital to see its Red Square, the Mausoleum, and its museums, ex-

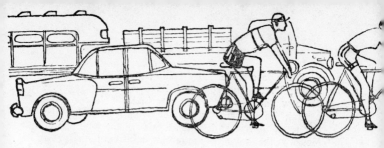

hibitions and theatres. The whole country joined in the celebrations of the city's 800th anniversary in 1947, for all the important events in Russia's history are closely associated with it, the heart and soul of centralized Muscovy.

Moscow's part in the First Russian Revolution of 1905-07 was particularly great. Its workers were the first to take up arms against tsarism. The December armed uprising in Moscow was the zenith of the popular 1905 revolution and profoundly influenced the development of revolutionary consciousness in the proletariat and the peoples of Russia as a whole. It caused the initial breach in the tsarist monarchy, which widened slowly but surely, undermining the old system.

Soviet power triumphed in Moscow on November 16, 1917, ten days after the outbreak of the Great October Socialist Revolution, and in March 1918 the Soviet Government headed by Lenin moved there from Petrograd. The red banner of the world's first socialist state was hoisted over the ancient Kremlin. On December 30, 1922, the First All-Union Congress of Soviets proclaimed the establishment of the Union of Soviet Socialist Republics, and ancient Moscow became the capital of the young multi-national Soviet state

When fascist Germany made its foul attack on the Soviet Union and directed its main blow against Moscow, the whole country rose in the defence of the capital. Reinforcements arrived from the Urals, the Far East, Siberia and Central Asia. In the environs of Moscow the sons of the entire multi-national state stood shoulder to shoulder, and hurled back the enemy. In December 1941 Hitler's armies suffered their first major defeat in the cruel Battle for Moscow, which exploded the myth about the invincibility of fascist arms. The Battle for Moscow was an important milestone in the struggle to clear the country of invaders.

Numerous new industrial plants, scientific and cultural institutions, and public works, have risen in Moscow in the first post-war decade. Blocks of dwelling houses are going up. Construction work is in progress on new subway lines, thoroughfares, sports grounds and stadiums. New restaurants, shops, laundries, workshops, cinemas are opening their doors to the public. Bus and trolley-bus lines are multiplying. The underground network of telephone lines and gas pipes, water and district-heating mains is being extended. The city is continuously growing. To give the reader an idea of the scale of Moscow's development, we present a brief account of the capital's reconstruction during the past 25 years.

It was only in the early thirties that the reconstruction and development of the city could be tackled in earnest to meet the requirements of rapid industrialization and the mounting demands of the city's growing population. The June 1931 Plenary Meeting of the Communist Party's Central Committee called on the Moscow Party Committee and the Moscow Soviet to deal with the urgent water supply, housing and transport problems.

Old Moscow had two water works. One, a fairly primitive conduit built in the 18th century, fed water from springs near the village of Bolshiye Mytishchi to a gravity canal, which conveyed it to hydrants in the city, where water-carriers filled their wooden casks. The other water supply system—the Rublyovo Water Works—was built in the early 19th century. It got its water from the Moskva River 50 kilometres (31 miles) outside city limits, near the village of Rublyovo, and conveyed it to a reservoir on the Vorobyovo (Lenin) Hills, from where it was fed to the city's water mains. The improvement of both water works in 1917 raised the water supply to a daily 13,000,000 buckets, or seven buckets per capita. Such was the state of affairs when Moscow entered the Soviet era.

Neither the reconstruction of the Rublyovo Water Works in 1931-34 and the construction of a water reservoir on the Istra River, nor the erection of the Cherepkovo aqueduct, solved the urgent water supply problem of the rapidly growing city, whose requirements promised to rise shortly to a daily hundred million buckets. The Moskva and its tributaries were obviously inadequate to fill the mounting needs of the capital. A vaster water source was required to feed the Moskva, and the Volga was made to serve the purpose. With the construction of the Moskva-Volga Canal the burning issue was solved. Four hydraulic pump-houses have been erected in the past twenty years, and one more is now under construction for the city's new south-western district. Today the aqueducts feeding water from the pump-houses to the city's water mains, and the mains themselves, total more than 2,000 kilometres (about 1,240 miles). In 1951-55 alone, nearly a thousand million rubles were spent on extending and improving Moscow's water works and sewerage.

The housing problem was solved chiefly by the erection of large dwelling projects in the former workers' settlements along Enthusiasts' Highway, in Dangauerovka, Usachovka, and Krasnaya Presnya, etc. The wretched wooden hovels and barracks in those localities gave place to tall new houses which, though modest and often severe in appearance, have bright, comfortable flats with all the modern amenities.

In 1935 the Central Committee of the C.P.S.U. and the Soviet Government adopted the General Plan of the Reconstruction of Moscow. It was a turning-point in the city's development. All the major building projects scattered throughout the various districts came under a single programme. The Government decision stipulated that the city's topography, shaped down the ages, should be preserved, and the thoroughfares and squares radically improved.

Radial and annular streets and side-streets are typical of Moscow's layout. Like all mediaeval cities, Moscow developed round the walls of a stronghold.

Subsequently, brick walls were also built round the merchants' quarter, known as Kitai-Gorod, which bordered the Kremlin in the east, between the Neglinka

and Moskva rivers, and, as the city extended north and west of the Kremlin, a new wall arose in the 16th century round the so-called Bely Gorod. It stretched along the line of what are now boulevards running from Kropotkinskiye Gate on the Moskva bank  to the mouth of the Yauza River near Ustyinsky Bridge. Another fortification, a timber wall this time, was erected in the late 16th century on a high earthwork rampart to girdle a new quarter which sprang up beyond the Bely Gorod walls. It is all these annular fortifications, which lent their circular shape to the streets laid around them, coupled with the radial roads converging toward the Kremlin, that formed the radial and annular pattern of Moscow's thoroughfares.

The Reconstruction Plan, so to speak, envisaged a "surgical" attack upon the maze of narrow and crooked streets, totally inadequate to meet the requirements of a modern city.

The task was to lend each square, thoroughfare, and embankment the appearance of a single architectural whole harmonizing with each other. The best features of classical and modern architecture, and up-to-date building techniques, were to be applied in housing development and the erection of public structures.

The Reconstruction Plan was drawn up with an eye to the city's future growth, and work was launched on a giant scale. The heart of the capital was the first objective. The ancient Kitai-Gorod wall was torn down, opening up Razin, Kuibishev and 25th October streets, and widening the adjacent thoroughfares. The petty chandler's shops round Moskvoretsky Bridge were removed. Red Square was cleared and improved, so that the walls and towers of the Kremlin, the bizarre contours of St. Basil's Cathedral, the Mausoleum, and the granite tribunes along the edge of the square formed a unique, unforgettable ensemble.

Before the outbreak of war in 1941 Okhotny Ryad, Manège Square, and such thoroughfares as Gorky Street, Bolshaya Kaluzhskaya Street, Pervaya Meshchanskaya Street, the Sadovaya streets along Sadovoye Circle, and Mozhaisk, Yaroslavl and Leningrad highways were entirely altered, or, rather, built anew.

Among the biggest buildings erected in the first five years after the adoption of the Reconstruction Plan were Moskva Hotel and the U.S.S.R. Council of Ministers building in Okhotny Ryad, the large dwelling-houses along Gorky Street, the new Lenin Library building, the Ministry of Light Industry building in Kirov Street, the Ministry of Agriculture building in Sadovo-Spasskaya Street, the Palace of Culture of the Likhachov Motor Works, the "Serp i Molot" Works club-house, the Palace of Culture in Fili, a number of institute buildings of the U.S.S.R. Academy of Sciences along Bolshaya Kaluzhskaya Street, the Institute of Experimental Medicine in Vsekhsvyatskoye, the Soviet Army Theatre, the Light Industry Technological Institute near Ustyinsky Bridge, the Moscow Non-Ferrous Metals Institute on Krimsky Val, etc.

In 1941-45, reconstruction work was largely interrupted by the war. But not all work stopped. It continued on the construction sites of new subway lines, and on the 843-kilometre (522.6-mile) gas pipe-line laid from Saratov to Moscow. Natural gas from Saratov considerably improved things. The economy derived from the use of cheap Saratov gas made good the expense of laying the pipe-line within thirty months after it was commissioned. Today Saratov is no longer Moscow's sole gas supplier. New gas conduits have been put into operation, such as the 1,300-kilometre (806-mile) Dashava-Kiev-Moscow line and the 1,310-kilometre (812-mile) Stavropol-Moscow line. Furthermore, a section of the projected Shchokino Gas Works in Tula Region, from where gas produced from coal mined in Moscow Region is pipe-lined to the capital, has also been put into operation.

Between 1935, when the Reconstruction Plan was adopted, and 1946, more than 13 thousand million rubles were expended on the reconstruction of Moscow.

The first five years after the war were highlighted by the stupendous Moscow University project on the Lenin Hills, and the erection of multi-storey buildings in Smolenskaya Square, Vosstaniye Square, Lermontov Square, Kalanchovskaya Street and Kotelnicheskaya Embankment. The multi-storey edifices have unquestionably added a touch of distinction to the city's architectonic. But they are not popular, because considerable floor space is wasted in them, and their maintenance is cumbrous and costly. No more buildings of that type are being built at present. Instead, architects are planning standard 4-, 6- and 8-storey buildings with two- and three-roomed family flats.

Reconstruction is carried on today under a General Plan for 1951-60. The Moscow General Plan Institute has been founded to elaborate upon problems bound up with reconstruction and development. Four of its

workshops draft lay-
outs and construc-
tion projects for each
of the capital's four
sectors—the South-
West, North-West,
North-East and South-
East. Another over-all
workshop supervises
their effort, co-ordinat-
ing it with the General
Reconstruction Plan of
Moscow. The Institute takes a hand in the improvement and development of all the capital's major public
works.

Today, mass construction of dwelling-houses and
public and cultural establishments has top priority in
the city's development. In 1956, for instance, completed
projects totalled 24,000,000 sq. metres (28.5 million sq.
yards). The Moscow housing development programme
of the Sixth Five-Year Plan (1956-60) stipulates the
erection of dwellings with a total floor space of another 11,000,000 sq. metres (11.3 million sq. yards). The
dwellings, and attendant shopping and cultural premises, no longer rise singly, and not even in blocks. They
rise in complete streets, built after a single pattern,
such as the Peschaniye streets, the streets of Oktyabrskoye Field and Perovo Field, the streets in the area of
Khoroshevskoye and Yaroslavl highways, and in the
neighbourhood of the new University building, the
U.S.S.R. Agricultural and Industrial Exhibition, and
elsewhere.

New houses also go up in the city's older streets
and squares, such as those in the Maryina Roshcha

and Zastava Ilyicha areas, in Bolshaya Serpukhovskaya Street, Danilovskaya Square, and the Moskva
and Yauza embankments.

Present-day housing projects are essentially different from those of former years. Moscow today has an
adequate building materials industry, which facili-
tates rapid building and the use of new prefabricated
section assembly methods. The day of tasteless embellishments, ornamental superstructures and colonnades,
porticos and architectural superfluities is over
and done with. Architects concentrate on improving
interior layouts and conveniences, striving to provide
comfortable, economical and rational types of dwellings.

The building of cultural and public establishments
is keeping pace with housing construction. Twenty-
five school buildings, kindergartens and crèches with
accommodations for 5,700, and six cinemas, were built
in 1956 alone, as well as hospitals, bath-houses, laundries, shops and catering establishments.

* * *

The capital's *public transport facilities* have been
radically reconstructed. As a matter of fact, one can
scarcely call it reconstruction. It was rather construction from scratch. A mere thirty years ago Muscovites
had only tramways and horse-driven cabs at their
disposal. Today they have the Metro, the trolley-bus,
bus, taxi and tram-car. Horse-driven cabs have completely vanished from the streets.

The Metro is a comfortable, rapid and economical
mode of travelling. The Metro passenger pays an
average fare of 8 kopeks per kilometre, the bus passenger—17 kopeks, the trolley-bus passenger—15 ko-

peks, and the tram-car passenger—9 kopeks. But the Metro has not, as yet, won first place among the city's transport facilities, because its network is not extensive enough. (For a detailed account of the Moscow Metro turn to p. 132.) At present the tramways carry the most people—more than a thousand million a year. Though the total length of the tramways has been reduced, new tracks have been laid in the outskirts of the city. More such lines are yet to be built in the Sixth Five-Year Plan period.

The trolley-bus has rapidly gained popularity. In the past twenty years its lines have increased in length from 22 to 393 kilometres (from 13.6 to 244 miles), and the number of vehicles from 57 to 941. An additional 132 kilometres (82 miles) of trolley-bus lines will be laid in the Sixth Five-Year Plan period, and 600 more trolley-buses will be put on the routes. In 1955 trolley-buses conveyed 665,000,000 passengers.

Buses are to make even greater progress. In the Sixth Five-Year Plan period one thousand more vehicles will be added to the present number, making a total of over 2,500. Furthermore, about 3,000 taxi-cabs ply the streets of Moscow.

In 1955, the number of passengers conveyed by Moscow's public conveyances totalled 3,175,000,000. This figure exceeds the figure of 20 years ago by 55 per cent. Apart from public conveyances, there is a great number of private and office cars.

The capital is linked with the rest of the country, and with the world, by all the modern means of communication.

It is the country's major railway junction. Ten railways radiate from it to all ends of the Soviet Union. The eleventh is the Okruzhnaya Railway, which girdles the city. The Moscow junction has eleven marshalling yards amply equipped with the latest handling mechanisms. The Okruzhnaya Railway serves as a link between these yards. What is more, Moscow is flanked in the east and west by detour tracks for transit freights.

The city has nine railway terminals: *Leningrad* Station of the Oktyabrskaya Railway, which links Moscow with Leningrad and Murmansk; *Yaroslavl* Station of the Severnaya Railway, which is the starting point of the Moscow-Vladivostok and Moscow-Peking routes; *Kazan* Station of the Moscow-Ryazan Railway, from which trains depart for Kazan, Ufa, Chelyabinsk, Magnitogorsk, Novorossiisk, Stalingrad, and the Central Asian republics of Kazakhstan, Kirghizia, Uzbekistan, Tajikistan and Turkmenistan; *Kursk* Station, with lines running to Azerbaijan, Georgia and Armenia, the Black Sea spas along the Caucasian and Crimean coasts, and the city of Gorky; *Paveletsk* Station, with lines to the Donets Coal Basin; *Kiev* Station of the Moscow-Kiev Railway, which is the starting point of routes to the Ukraine and Moldavia, and to the station of Chop on the Hungarian and Czechoslovak border; *Byelorussia* Station of the Western Railway, with routes to Minsk, Brest, Kaliningrad, Warsaw and Berlin; *Savyolovo* Station of the Severnaya Railway, from which trains follow the Moskva Canal to Shcherbakov in the upper reaches of the Volga; and *Riga* Station of the Kalinin Railway, which links Moscow with Riga, the Latvian capital.

Suburban railways are serviced almost entirely by electric trains.

Automobile Transport. The railway is being increasingly supplemented by motor transport. The Ryazan, Shcholkovo, Gorky, Yaroslavl, Dmitrov, Leningrad, Volokolamsk, Rublyovo, Minsk, Borovsk, Narofominsk, Kaluga, Podolsk, and Kashira highways diverge from the city in all directions. A ring road is under construction some 18 kilometres (11 miles) out of the city, to link all these highways. That will clear the crowded Moscow thoroughfares of transit traffic, which at present daily amounts to about 60,000 lorries and cars.

Comfortable buses ply between Moscow and other cities, such as Simferopol and Yalta in the Crimea, Minsk and Kharkov, etc.

After the construction of the Moscow Canal the *Moskva River* has become a full-fledged city artery. The plan of the canal which connects the Moskva with the Volga was approved in late 1932. Four years and eight months later a fleet of passenger steamers, the first to traverse the new canal and the Moskva, approached the Kremlin on May 2, 1937. On July 15 of the same year the canal was opened to general shipping, and in 1947, the year of Moscow's 800th anniversary, it was named Moscow Canal.

The canal begins at the village of Ivankovo, Kalinin Region, where a large reservoir 120 kilometres (74

miles) long and 8 kilometres (5 miles) wide, known as the "Moskovskoye Sea," formed after the erection of a dam and hydroelectric power station. It is also the site of the forward sluice. Eight more sluices dot the course,  comprising a kind of staircase to raise and lower vessels en route to and from Moscow. Several reservoirs have been built along the way. The canal terminates beyond Moscow at the Perervinskaya Dam. It is a complicated system of sluices, dams, pumping stations, hydropower houses, spillways, floodgates, lighthouses, piers and landing-stages, etc., totalling about 200 different structures.

The Moscow and Volga-Don canals have linked Moscow with the White, Baltic, Caspian, Azov and Black seas.

The city has three river ports: the North Port on Khimki Reservoir, the West Port in Fili, and the South Port near the Likhachov Motor Works. These handle the bulk of incoming and outgoing water-borne freight. The ports are equipped with up-to-date handling mechanisms—powerful cranes, pneumatic transfer machines, belt conveyers and loaders, etc. Two landing-stages serve the passenger lines to Ufa, Stalingrad, Astrakhan, Rostov and other river ports. In summer, suburban and local passenger steamers ply up and down the Moskva and the Canal.

The transfigured Moskva wanted a new setting.

Granite embankments and imposing stairways down the banks were erected in next to no time. Ten new bridges across the river and the drainage canal were built in two years (1936-38). The new bridges are almost all substantially higher, wider and longer than the old. They span both the river and the embankments, eliminating intersections and making for non-stop motor traffic along the river banks.

All of them, save Krimsky Bridge, are arch bridges. Bolshoi Krasnokholmsky Bridge (Engineer Vakhurkin and Architect Kokorin) has the biggest arch span (160 metres, or about 525 ft.) and is one of the world's longest of its kind.

Airlines link Moscow with many cities of the U.S.S.R. and a number of foreign capitals. The city has two passenger airports—in Bykovo, 32 km. (20 miles) south-east, and in Vnukovo, 24 km. (15 miles) south-west of Moscow.

The Soviet Union has a vast network of airlines. Fairly extensive air connections are available with foreign countries. There are direct air routes between Moscow and Bucharest, Sofia, Tirana, Belgrade, Budapest, Warsaw, Prague, Vienna, Berlin, Helsinki, Copenhagen, Stockholm, Kabul, Ulan-Bator, Peking and Phyöngyang. The Moscow-Paris airline, with a change in Prague, is operated jointly with France, and the Delhi-Moscow line, with a change in Kabul, jointly with Indian airlines. Some routes of the Soviet Passenger Air Fleet are worked by the latest jet passenger aircraft.

* * *

Moscow is one of the country's major industrial centres. Even at the close of the last century it had a

fairly great number of factories and plants. But present-day Moscow is by rights an entirely new industrial city. Its industries were reconstructed and extended in line with the industrialization of the whole country.

Engineering holds a leading place in the city's industries. Its major engineering works play a big part in developing and improving Soviet industry. They are, so to speak, the industrial and designing laboratories of a good many of the country's plants.

Among the city's major undertakings are the "Serp i Molot" High-Grade Steel Works, the Kirov "Dynamo" Electrical Engineering Works, the "Krasny Proletary" and Orjonikidze Machine-Tool Works, the Likhachov Motor Works, and others.

The Moscow industries produce up-to-date machinery and instruments: general-purpose hydro-copying semi-automatic machines, improved gear-grinding machines, and instruments utilizing radio-active elements. The Orjonikidze Works puts out entire automobile and agricultural machinery production lines.

Moscow has large-scale consumer goods industries. Its textile plants, together with those of Moscow Region, hold a prominent place in the country's over-all textile output, manufacturing 30 per cent of all cotton fabrics, 55 per cent of all woollen fabrics and 46 per cent of all silk fabrics produced in the Soviet Union.

The Mikoyan Meat Plant, the Dairy Plant which processes 600 tons of milk daily to produce 500 thousand bottles of kefir, cream, and whole milk, and the "Krasny Oktyabr" and "Bolshevik" confectioneries, etc., are the major enterprises of the Moscow food industry.

In the Fifth Five-Year Plan period Moscow's over-all industrial output rose 70.3 per cent, the rolled stock output 24 per cent, the automobile and machine tool output 50 per cent, and the output of ball bearings and electro-motors almost 100 per cent. In the same period the output of woollen fabrics increased 54 per cent and silk fabrics 160 per cent.

Under the Sixth Five-Year Plan the city's industrial output is to rise about 65 per cent.

* * *

Moscow is the centre of Soviet science and culture. It is the seat of the U.S.S.R. Academy of Sciences with its numerous institutes, laboratories and other scientific institutions. Six specialized academies are centred in Moscow: the academies of agricultural and medical sciences, the Academy of Building and Architecture, the Academy of Arts, the R.S.F.S.R. Academy of Pedagogical Sciences, and the Public Utilities Academy of the R.S.F.S.R.

The capital has 448 research institutions and 70 establishments of higher learning employing over 14,000 professors and training men and women in almost all professions required by the national economy. The leading place is held by Moscow State University.

Moscow is famous for its drama, opera and ballet. The Moscow Art Theatre, and the Bolshoi and Maly theatres, are veritable pearls of the Russian stage. After the Revolution many new theatres sprang up, rapidly winning widespread popularity. Among them are Vakhtangov Theatre, Mayakovsky Theatre, Mossoviet Theatre, Central Theatre of the Soviet Army, Central Transport Theatre, Sergei Obraztsov's Central Puppet Theatre, the Children's Theatre and the Stanislavsky and Nemirovich-Danchenko Musical Theatre.

No acquaintance with Moscow's theatrical traditions would be complete without a visit to the Bakhrushin Theatrical Museum (12/31, Zatsepsky Val). Alexei Bakhrushin (1865-1929), a wealthy Moscow businessman and opera and ballet lover, who was long and intimately associated with the Maly Theatre, started his collection of "things theatrical" at an early age. In the sixty years of its existence the museum has accumulated upwards of 200,000 photographs and negatives, 20,000 oil, ink and sculptural portraits of outstanding men and women connected with the stage, and upwards of 30,000 sketches of stage settings and costumes.

The Moscow Chaikovsky Conservatoire is the country's leading school of music. Besides, Moscow has many symphony and variety orchestras, song and dance ensembles, the Pyatnitsky Russian Folk Choir, Igor Moiseyev's Folk Dance Ensemble, and the "Beryozka" Dance Ensemble directed by Nadezhdina.

Moscow has 47 art, history and science museums; 941 public libraries, including the Lenin Library, which is one of the world's largest; many houses of culture and factory clubs; and a number of professional clubs for intellectuals, such as the Art Workers' Club, the Actors' Club, the Journalists' Club, The Writers' Club, the Scientists' Club, the Medical Club, the Club of Engineers and Technicians, the Teachers' Club, etc.

Several motion picture studios, radio and television broadcasting stations, dozens of newspapers and journals, and a great many publishing houses are centred in Moscow.

Recreation. In summer the city's parks and gardens are popular resorts of recreation and entertainment. The Moskva with its eleven beaches and splendid boating facilities, and the delightful suburban woods, fields, brooks, water reservoirs, and particularly the Klyazma Reservoir with its Bay of Radost (Good Cheer), attract sportsmen, bathers, fishermen and nature lovers.

The city expends up to 10 million rubles annually for the maintenance and improvement of its ten recreation parks and seventeen children's parks. The largest and most popular *Gorky Recreation Park* is described on page 80. Two other Moscow parks— Izmailovo and Sokolniki—which are omitted from our routes, merit some attention.

Luxuriant *Izmailovo Park*, the remnant of a onetime dense Moscow forest, runs like a broad ribbon alongside Enthusiasts' Highway. In the dim past it was inhabited by bears, wolves, foxes, and even elks and deer.

In the 17th century it was the site of Tsar Alexei Mikhailovich's countryside residence, whose ruins stand to this day. The estate comprised a wooden palace, a five-domed cathedral, a gateway with towers and belfry, a pond and several dams. It had gardens of unequalled beauty. Peter I[1] passed his childhood in Izmailovo. After Alexei's death the estate fell into disrepair, and passed into total oblivion after the capital was transferred from Moscow to Petersburg.

As capitalism developed the Izmailovo district and its adjoining workers' settlements of Preobrazhenskaya, Semyonovskaya and Cherkizovo became a quarter of many industrial plants and handicrafts, chiefly cotton spinning mills, weavers' workshops, bleacheries, etc.

In our day a splendid recreation park has been laid out on an area of over 1,000 hectares (2,470 acres) of the surviving woodland. The front part of the park has various recreation facilities, the "Trudoviye Rezervy" Sports Society's stadium, and large ponds. Farther on is a magnificent pine forest, in which evergreen pines and firs mingle with white birches, maples, larches and lime-trees. The well-kept woodland is cut by lanes and paths, and dotted with numerous glades of camomiles and bluebells. A mere twenty minutes' walk from the Metro one has

the impression of being in the heart of a thick forest. A large nursery is located on the park grounds.

Sokolniki Recreation Park north of Izmailovo has an area of 600 hectares (1,480 acres). It occupies a tract flanking Moscow on the north—another remnant of old-time forestland where, in days gone by, the tsars pursued their sport of falconry, from which it derives its name (*sokol* being the Russian for falcon).

In the mid-19th century the City Duma bought the forest and turned it into a city park with seven Radial clearings diverging from the main Circle. It has been a favourite outdoor recreation ground ever since. From the late 19th century Sokolniki has been associated with the revolutionary movement of the Moscow proletariat. It was a "green underground," as it were. Workers held their May Day meetings and illegal gatherings in its cloistered seclusion, and in 1905 detachments of armed workers came there to practise revolver shooting in preparation of the armed uprising.

After the Revolution, Sokolniki became a popular recreation park. It has indoor and outdoor skating-rinks, and skiing facilities, and is the site of the Soviet Army Club Stadium and the stadium of the Spartak Sports Society. Sokolniki Park is distinctive for its appearance of deliberate desolation. Even the flower-beds are haphazardly placed in picturesque clumps, devoid of the usual geometrical symmetry. It has luxuriant tracts of woodland, in which oaks mingle with elm-trees, birches, chestnut-trees, limes, ash-trees, firs, cedar-trees, pines and spruces. Furthermore, it has its own tree nursery.

The Park merges gradually with the woodlands of Pogonno-Losiny Island, which, with its famous Alexeyevskaya Preserve and its mighty century-old pines, sprawls over an area of 2,000 hectares (4,942 acres) north-east of Moscow.

* * *

This Guide does not presume to give an exhaustive account of Moscow's history, culture and economy. The author merely set himself the task of selecting facts and figures that would afford a general, more or less clear, picture of Moscow. The routes presented in the Guide take the reader through the city's principal quarters, and encompass a fairly large, representative part of the city, and particularly its landmarks.

THE KREMLIN

The striking contours of the ancient Kremlin, a mediaeval citadel, have come to be a veritable symbol of Soviet Moscow. The Kremlin walls, shaped like an isosceles triangle, encompass an area of 26 hectares (64.2 acres), where the most ancient relics of Russian history and culture have been preserved to our time. It was here, eight centuries ago, that Moscow came into being at the confluence of the Moskva River and its tributary, the Neglinka, atop a hill on the left bank. In the dim past this was a densely wooded, southernmost outskirt of the Suzdal Principality. Its population engaged in farming, hunting and fishing.

Prince Yury Dolgoruky of Rostov-Suzdal[2] was attracted by the advantages it offered in military combat, located as it was upon the high, steep bank of the Moskva River, and bordered on the north-west by the Neglinka with its swampy banks. In 1147, Yury Dolgoruky and his men-at-arms pitched their princely camp there, and held a feast in tribute to Prince Svyatoslav of Novgorod-Seversky, Dolgoruky's friend and ally. In describing the event, the ancient chronicler identifies the site of that auspicious occasion as "Moskov" for the first time, and it is on the strength of his authentic account that 1147 is taken as the year when Moscow was founded.

In 1156, fortified timber walls were erected round the small hilltop settlement, which had by then become a princely estate. But owing to incessant wars with its neighbours, and particularly the Mongol Tatars, the Moscow Kremlin had to be reinforced. Prince Ivan I (1325-40), better known as Kalita (meaning "money-bag"), a shrewd and vigorous ruler, extended the Kremlin grounds and erected a new wall of oak logs up to a metre thick. But even this, it soon developed, was not enough. The Tatars continued to menace the Moscow Principality, and in 1367, under the rule of Dmitry Ivanovich, later named Dmitry Donskoi for his victory over the Tatars at Kulikovo Field on the Don, the Kremlin was enlarged to nearly its present size, and fortified with stone walls.

In another 120 years, under Grand Duke Ivan III (1462-1505), the brick walls that stand today were erected on a stone rampart. By that time, Moscow had become the capital of the centralized Russian state. Ivan III sought to turn the Kremlin into a first-class fortress worthy of Muscovy's rising prestige. The Kremlin towers were topped by grim-looking battlements. The present-day ornamental tent-like superstructures were added to the towers only after the

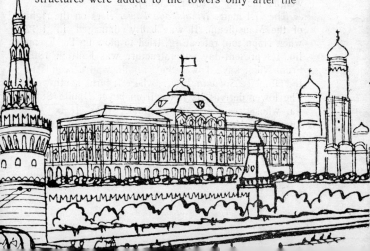

Kremlin lost its importance as a citadel in the 17th century. The towers and walls of the Kremlin underwent repeated repairs, but it was only in 1947 that large-scale restoration work was undertaken. The white stone base of the Kremlin walls, the gilded weather vanes, and the coloured glazed tiles regained their original splendour. Deteriorated brick and stone parts were replaced.

The Moscow Kremlin has 20 towers. The most striking *Spasskaya Tower,* regarded as the main portal to the Kremlin, rises in Red Square on the left of the Mausoleum. Built in 1491, it is the tallest of the twenty, being 67.3 metres (220 feet) high. In 1851 the clock, whose chimes are daily heard at midnight over Radio Moscow, was mounted in Spasskaya Tower. In 1917, during the battles for Soviet power, the clock was damaged by artillery shells. Some time later, by Lenin's order, it was restored and its musical chimes altered. The huge, unwieldy clockwork and the bells are mounted in the two upper storeys. The largest bell strikes on the hour, the others strike on the quarter-hour and ring the chimes. The biggest bell, cast in 1769 by the fine Russian modeller, Semyon Mozzhukhin, weighs 135 poods (over 2 tons).

The 67.1-metre *Nikolskaya Tower* rises on the right of the Mausoleum. It was badly damaged in 1812 when Napoleon, retreating, tried to blow up the Kremlin. Its present-day superstructure was built in 1816. From Nikolskaya Tower the Kremlin wall descends to the 60-metre *Sobakin Tower,* where it turns south-west. The tower derives its name from boyar Danila Sobaka, whose residence it originally was. It is also known as *Uglovaya Arsenalnaya,* because it adjoins

the Arsenal building, whose long façade is in plain
view from Manège Square.

The western wall of the Kremlin has two
gate towers—Troitskaya and Borovitskaya. *Troitskaya
Tower* is much like Spasskaya in appearance, but its
architectural embellishments are less lavish, and it is
three metres lower. A handsome stone bridge leads
from the Troitskaya Tower gateway over the promenades of Alexandrovsky Garden to the openwork
Kutafya Tower, which once served as a bridgehead.
Recent archaeological excavations at the foot of the
tower revealed a good many objects that supplemented our knowledge of the Kremlin's history.

Borovitskaya Tower perpetuated the memory of a
dense forest, on whose former site it was built (*bor*
being the Russian for forest). It stands within the
limits of Yury Dolgoruky's estate, and its 50.7-metre
frame (1490) is reminiscent of a staired pyramid.

In 1488 a tower was erected at the extreme end
of the Kremlin promontory. In 1633, ingenious crafts-
men raised water from the tower-well and conveyed
it along a chute to the Kremlin palaces and gardens.
It has been called *Vodovzvodnaya* (water-raising)
Tower ever since. Its shape is reminiscent of a chess
rook, and is not devoid of grace and buoyancy in
spite of its 58.7 metres.

The entire southern wall of the Kremlin triangle
is in plain view from Sofiiskaya Embankment. It was
the first to be erected, because Moscow was most vulnerable on the south to incessant enemy, particularly
Tatar, raids. Standing in front of the British Embassy building, you face *Tainitskaya Tower* (1485), the
point where the erection of the Kremlin walls was
begun. A secret underground passage was built from

the tower to the riverside to ensure the fortress's
water supply in the event of a siege. The eastern end
of the southern wall merges with the 46.2-metre *Bek-
lemishevskaya Tower,* built in 1487, whose original appearance has been best preserved in subsequent alterations. Its peaked top was built in 1680.

Konstantino-Yeleninskaya Tower is the next in
line. It had a gateway, opening upon a street running
along the foot of the Kremlin hill. On the outer side
the moat was spanned by a bridge. In the 16th and
17th centuries the tower was used as a prison and
became known to the people as *Pytoshnaya* (torture)
Tower.

In 1937, five Kremlin towers (Spasskaya, Nikolskaya, Borovitskaya, Troitskaya and Vodovzvodnaya)
were adorned with ruby stars, each of a different size.
The span between the tips of the smallest star mounted
on Vodovzvodnaya Tower is 3 metres, and of those
mounted on Spasskaya and Nikolskaya towers, 3.75
metres. The stars are mounted on special ball bearings and yield freely to the pressure of the wind. A
special optical device and unique electric bulbs provide
uniform lighting, making the stars clearly visible at
great distances day and night.

*are 3' bigger & *

and are

In 1954 after the fall of Stalin & Beria, Malenkov opened the Kremlin to the public & now thousand daily are able to see the treasures & buildings in which Stalin had enveloped himself.

The Moscow Kremlin is a signal monument of Russian culture. Its palaces and cathedrals of unique ancient national architecture, its works of art and ikonography, its peerless collection of ancient arms, royal regalia, the tsars' personal belongings, precious utensils, objects of religious worship, etc., are of unusual interest. Open to visitors, the Kremlin is inspected by several thousand of them daily.

Bolshoi Kremlyovsky (Grand Kremlin) *Palace*, by K. A. Ton, was built in 1838-49 on an eminence of the Kremlin Hill, facing the Moskva River. It is ~~120 me-tres~~ 400 ou" long, and its double-clearance halls on the first storey give it the outer appearance of a three-storey building.

It has many spacious halls, ~~whose artistic orna-mentation and lavish appointments are reflected in the patterns and colours of~~ decoration ribbons. The largest, Georgievsky Hall, is dedicated to the victories of Russian arms; marble tablets on its walls bear the names of military units, and of officers, decorated with the Georgievsky Cross. The hall is adorned with eighteen spiral zinc columns topped by sculptured figures by I. Vitali, the ~~eminent~~ sculptor. Magnificent ornaments cover the vault, and the parquet floor-ing, laid of twenty precious wood species, is remin-iscent of a gorgeous carpet. The white ~~gala~~ hall is lighted by six bronze chandeliers, each weighing more than a ton.

The other monumental assembly hall in the palace was reconstructed ~~in our day~~ from the former Alexandrovsky and Andreyevsky halls. It is here that the Communist Party of the Soviet Union holds its congresses, and that the Supreme Soviets of the U.S.S.R. and R.S.F.S.R. convene. All-Union conferences of the Party and Government leadership with representatives of industry, agriculture, literature and science, are also held in this hall.

The Grand Kremlin Palace is rectangular in shape, and stands on the site of the former princely estate. The surviving structures of the estate, built as far back as the 15th century, are now enclosed by the new palace, whose square inner courtyard they occupy. The palace is adjoined by *Zolotaya Tsaritsina Palata*, the *Terems*, and *Granovitaya Palata* (Hall of Many Facets). The latter was built by the Italian architects Marco Ruffo and Pietro Solari in 1487-91 in the style of Moscow and Novgorod residences. Its façade is finished in small, faceted stones, from which it derives its name. It is the only surviving assembly hall of the original Kremlin Palace, the scene of gala receptions, and long the throne-room of the Russian tsars. Granovitaya Palata communicates with the Grand Palace by a corridor called "Svyatiye Seni" (Holy Passage). A small chamber concealed from view is situated above it, known as "Tainik" (Secret Chamber). From this chamber tsarinas and tsarevnas watched official ceremonies, which they were not allowed to attend, through a latticed window, screened from prying eyes by silken drapings. There was much to look at from behind the silken screen: gala receptions of foreign ambassadors, initiations of metropolitans, sittings of boyar dumas, and other

[handwritten margin note:] too naturally much Italian influence & in this above of eastern pattern looks a very uncomfortable

solemn acts of state. Ivan the Terrible[3] celebrated the conquest of Kazan (1552) in Granovitaya Palata, and Peter I[1] his victory over the Swedes at Poltava (1709).

The residential sections of the old Kremlin Palace, the so-called "Terems," contrast sharply with the ostentatious Granovitaya Palata for their intimacy and comfort. After the big fire they were built anew in 1636, this time of brick instead of wood, and adorned with richly carved stone window-frames. The Terems have no gala chambers. Their rooms are small, and the coloured sheets of mica in the windows diffuse a pleasant half-light. The appointments include costly carved furniture, carpets, table-cloths, and diverse colourful, gold-embroidered tapestry.

One of the most remarkable museums in the country—*Oruzheinaya Palata* (Armoury)—is located in the Kremlin. Its exhibits include objects of great historical and cultural value, collected down the ages in the repositories of the Moscow princes and the tsar's court. Six hundred years ago first mention is made in Ivan Kalita's will of some of the treasures that later served as the nucleus of the present collection. As the Russian centralized state took shape and Moscow's predominance asserted itself, fabulous riches came to the hands of the Grand Dukes of Muscovy—precious stones, gold and silver objects, richly adorned arms and accoutrements, rare fabrics and embroideries, lavish utensils, and royal regalia, etc.

The unique, inimitable art of the old Russian masters is particularly striking. Oruzheinaya Palata holds the only collection in the world revealing the superb art, the high level of culture, and the excellent taste of Moscow gold- and silversmiths of the 16th and 17th centuries.

A great many exhibits are associated with events and individuals renowned in Russian history. The visitor will see the ancient Cap of Monomakh, the tsar's crown which Ivan III placed on the head of his grandson Dmitry in 1498; Prince Pyotr Shuisky's coat of mail, which passed to Ivan the Terrible after his death and which the latter presented to Yermak, the conqueror of Siberia; the helmet of Tsar Mikhail Romanov, founder of the last tsarist dynasty; the precious upholstery of Boris Godunov's[4] throne, his golden ring with the sign of the cross, adorned with black, blue and green enamel, pearls, and sapphires; the kaftans of Peter I,[1] the golden brocade church garb of Patriarch Nikon (mid-17th century), whose pearls alone weighed up to 20 kilogrammes; the carriage presented by Queen Elizabeth of Britain to Tsar Boris Godunov, and many other remarkable exhibits.

Among the presents of foreign embassies particular attention is drawn to the collection of English silverware, made by London silversmiths of the 16th-17th centuries. The collection is of extraordinary historical and artistic value. No study of English silver of that time is complete without it, since there is no collection of its kind elsewhere, even in Britain.

Oruzheinaya Palata was built specially as a museum in 1851 after the design by K. Ton.

On the east side, the Grand Palace is adjoined by *Blagoveshchensky* (Annunciation) *Cathedral*—the chapel of Ivan III, erected by Pskov builders in 1484-89 in the style of early-Moscow architecture. It is 20.3 metres high, 13.6 metres long and 10.2 metres wide. The cathedral suffered considerably in one of the great Kremlin fires, but was restored in 1564 under Ivan the Terrible. Its galleries were roofed, and new domes were erected. The formerly modest chapel was thus turned into a picturesque nine-domed cathedral. Its ikons are rare objects of art by such renowned ancient Russian artists as Andrei Rublyov,[5] Feofan Grek, Prokhor of Gorodets, etc. The portals of the chapel are adorned with exquisite carvings in stone, and the floor of the church is laid with slabs of Ural jasper.

Another relic of Russian architecture, *Arkhangelsky Cathedral*, was built in 1505-09 by architect Aleviso Novy. It is 34 metres high, 37.6 metres long, and more than 21 metres wide. It holds the burial-vaults of the Moscow grand dukes and tsars. The tombs line the walls of the cathedral, and there are mural portraits of Ivan Kalita, Ivan III, Ivan the Terrible, Fyodor Ivanovich, Alexei Mikhailovich and others. A carved white-stone marquee rises over the tomb of Ivan the Terrible's son, Tsarevich Dmitry,[4] killed in Uglich. His coffin was installed in the cathedral in 1606. The murals date from 1666, and many of the paintings from the 15th-18th centuries. The original murals, which are of extraordinary artistic and historical value, were restored in 1954-55.

The famous *Uspensky* (Assumption) *Cathedral* towers in the centre of the Kremlin triangle. It was

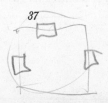

with this magnificent edifice, meant to symbolize the power of the united Russian state, that Grand Duke Ivan III began the reconstruction of the Kremlin. It was built by Aristotle Fioravanti, the outstanding Italian architect. The gifted architect designed it in the style of the 12th-century cathedral in the town of Vladimir, drawing skilfully upon the unique mannerisms of the Russian masters. The main cathedral in Muscovy, it was completed in 1479 on Kremlin Cathedral Square, and is 38 metres high, almost 24 metres wide, and 35.5 metres long, occupying an area of 842 sq. metres. Its walls and columns are covered with murals, the central ikonostas is adorned with engraved silver trimmings, and it contains the exquisitely carved walnut throne of Ivan the Terrible. Uspensky Cathedral was the coronation church of the Russian tsars, and the tombs of metropolitans and patriarchs who played a big part in the affairs of Muscovy, particularly during its inception, are installed in it.

The *Bell-Tower of Ivan the Great* is of special interest. This magnificent edifice is part and parcel of everything associated with the Kremlin and Moscow. It is the pivot of the Kremlin ensemble. The lower part of the tower was erected in 1505-08. The belfry and chapel were added later, and the upper gallery of the belfry (81 metres) was built by Boris Godunov[4] in 1600, which fact is inscribed upon the cupola in three lines of gilded letters. The cupola, cross and inscription were freshly gilded in 1955.

Two unique examples of the art of ancient Russian founders—the Tsar-Bell and Tsar-Cannon—flank the Bell-Tower of Ivan the Great.

Tsar-Bell was cast by Ivan Matorin and his son Mikhail in 1735. The bell weighs 200 tons. It is ~~5~~ metres 87 centimetres high and has a diameter of ~~6~~ metres 60 centimetres. During the 1737 fire the bell fell from its scaffolding, and a fragment weighing more than 11 tons broke off. It was only 100 years later that the bell was raised out of the pit it made in falling, and was installed on a granite base, upon which it stands to this day, having become one of the landmarks of the Kremlin. *Tsar-Cannon* was cast in 1586 by Andrei Chokhov, master of the cannon yard. It weighs 40 tons, its barrel is ~~upwards of~~ 5 metres in ~~length~~ and its calibre is 89 centimetres.

In the mid-18th century two large edifices were added to the Kremlin ensemble. One was the Arsenal, whose façade is lined with the tubes of cannon captured from Napoleon's armies. The other was the building of the former Senate. The latter ~~is an outstanding~~ architectural monument, built by the famous Moscow architect, Matvei Kazakov.[6] Its dome is plainly visible from Red Square, topped by the National Flag of the Soviet Union. It has been the seat of the Soviet Government since ~~the latter~~ removed from Petrograd to Moscow. V. I. Lenin's study-room was located in the building, and so was his residence, which has now been turned into a home-museum. The appointments in Lenin's study have been preserved untouched to this day. A replica of the study is on display at the Lenin Museum.

The Kremlin attracts crowds of visitors, who come to see the priceless relics of Russian history and culture. In the twelvemonth from July 1955 to July 1956 it was visited by 5,000,000 people, including visitors from fifty foreign countries.

Since the Kremlin was opened in 1954 it has been estimated that about 5 million people visit it each year.

RED SQUARE—REVOLUTION SQUARE—SVERDLOV SQUARE—OKHOTNY RYAD

Red Square is one of the finest open places in Moscow and the scene of many momentous events of Russian history. In 1917, the final battles of the Moscow proletariat for Soviet power were fought in Red Square, and the fighters who lost their lives in them are buried in a common grave at the foot of the Kremlin wall.

Red Square is the point of convergence of working people's demonstrations. On holidays columns of working people pour into the square in a broad stream from Gorky Street and Manège Square; filing past the tribune on the Mausoleum, they are greeted by the Party and Government leadership. Soviet Army parades take place in Red Square on May 1 and November 7.

The Mausoleum of Vladimir Ilyich Lenin, founder of the Communist Party and the Soviet state, is in Red Square. The sarcophagus with the body of Joseph Vissarionovich Stalin is also installed in the Mausoleum. The Mausoleum, built by Academician A. V. Shchusev, is faced with black and grey labradorite and red Ukrainian granite. Higher up, granite columns support the slab of red Karelian porphyry which tops the Mausoleum.

Urns with the remains of distinguished Communist Party leaders and Soviet statesmen are immured in the Kremlin wall. Their names are carved upon marble plaques. Sculptured portraits of M. I. Kalinin,[7] F. E. Dzerzhinsky,[8] Y. M. Sverdlov,[9] M. V. Frunze,[10] and A. A. Zhdanov,[11] by U.S.S.R. People's Artist S. D. Merkulov, are mounted on granite pedestals before the respective tombs.

The history of Red Square is bound up closely with the development of Moscow. The square was a major trading place, known as red, a word whose earlier meaning connoted beauty. It was the point of convergence of highways leading through Moscow from the major townships of ancient Rus, and the scene of ceaseless, noisy and brisk commerce. In the 16th century the square was separated from the Kremlin by a deep moat running alongside the Kremlin wall; bridges spanned the moat at Spasskiye and Nikolskiye gates. On the south the square descended steeply to the river, and on the edge of the slope ("lob" in Russian) opposite Spasskiye Gate was an enclosed stone

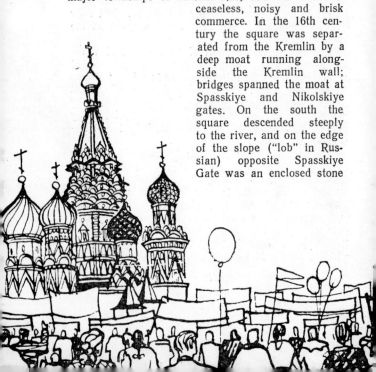

elevation—"Lobnoye Mesto"—from which the tsar's ukases and sentences were read to the people. The eastern end of the square was occupied by an emporium of stalls and shops.

Whatever major political events unfolded in the city, they were inevitably consummated in Red Square. That is natural, because it was in the immediate neighbourhood of the Kremlin—the political, administrative and ecclesiastical centre of Moscow and the principality. Furthermore, the people sought safety from enemy raids behind the Kremlin's sturdy walls. Red Square has on several occasions been the site of popular vengeance against the hated feudalistic boyars. It has also been the site of public executions. In 1671, for instance, Stepan Razin,[12] leader of a peasant uprising, was executed in Red Square, and in 1698 Peter I executed here the *streltsi,* a class of citizens and merchants who rendered hereditary military service to the tsar, and who opposed his progressive innovations. The execution of the *streltsi* inspired the historical canvas by Surikov, the famed Russian artist, on display at the Tretyakov Gallery ("The Execution of the *Streltsi*").

In 1713-14 the capital was transferred to Petersburg (now Leningrad),

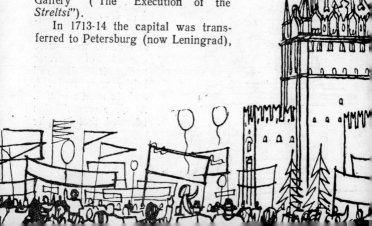

and Red Square lost its importance. Only in 1917 it again became an arena of political struggle. The battles for possession of the Kremlin took place near Nikolskiye Gate. Armed Moscow workers and revolutionary soldiers crushed the resistance of counter-revolutionary officers and military cadets holding the Kremlin, and consummated the triumph of Soviet power in Moscow.

* * *

On the south side of Red Square is *St. Basil's Cathedral*, a masterpiece of Russian architecture built in 1555-60 by Ivan the Terrible[3] to commemorate the conquest of Kazan. Its design, by the stone-masons Postnik and Barma, follows traditional Russian forms. The base has the shape of a cross, ends pointing to the four winds. Four chapels stand at these ends, alternating with four lower structures. The tallest chapel with a marquee-like top rises in the centre. The gifted architects did not repeat themselves in a single dome, or ornament, of this picturesque set, yet achieved a commanding and majestic whole.

In 1954 the magnificent edifice was restored. Its walls were cleared of diverse sediments, damaged bricks were replaced, and the must removed. A close examination revealed that in spite

of its 400 years the edifice was still extremely strong. In clearing the walls, the restorationists discovered layers of vivid, highly durable paint dating back to the 16th century. At present, the original colouring of the cathedral has been reproduced.

St. Basil's Cathedral is affiliated with the History Museum.

The *Monument of Kuzma Minin*[13] *and Dmitry Pozharsky*[14] has been transferred to the grounds of the cathedral from a near-by site in Red Square. The statue, by Ivan Martos, is cast in bronze. It was unveiled in 1818. The sculptural group shows Kuzma Minin, patriot and Nizhny-Novgorod merchant, exhorting Prince Dmitry Pozharsky to liberate Moscow from the Polish invaders (1612). Two ornaments in bas-relief adorn the pedestal. One shows donations being collected for Pozharsky's volunteer army, and the other, the expulsion of the invaders from the capital.

On the east side of Red Square are two large buildings—the former upper and middle emporiums. The middle emporium, between Kuibishev and Razin streets, was built in 1901, and is now occupied by government offices. The upper emporium, between Kuibishev and October 25th streets, was built in 1893, and was at the time one of the largest emporiums in Europe. In 1953, after a major reconstruction, it became the site of *GUM,* the largest department store in the Soviet Union. GUM rapidly became a centre of attraction not only to Muscovites, but out-of-town visitors as well. It is crowded from morning to night, selling every variety of consumer goods. It has its own custom workshops making suits, overcoats, dresses and footwear. Its staff totals 4,000. The store

is equipped with powerful refrigerators, heating installations and up-to-date air-conditioning, which effects
three total changes of air in an hour.

On the north side of Red Square is the massive
History Museum building, flanked by two thoroughfares, the left one connecting Red Square with Manège Square, and the right one with Revolution
Square and Gorky Street. The thoroughfares were laid
after the brick Kitai-Gorod wall was torn down.

The Kitai-Gorod wall encompassed the former business quarter—a fairly large area from Arsenalnaya
Tower in the Kremlin wall, across Revolution Square
and Teatralny Lane to Dzerzhinsky Square, and south
tc the Moskva, following the embankment to Moskvoretsky Bridge. In the thirties almost all of it was
removed under the Moscow Reconstruction Plan, only
small sections surviving along the fringe of Revolution Square and running from Nogin Square to the embankment.

We leave Red Square by the thoroughfare right of
the History Museum and come to the *Central Lenin
Museum* in *Revolution Square.* The museum's nineteen
exposition halls display originals and photographs of
documents, manuscripts, books, periodicals, leaflets,
pictures, paintings, sculptures, objects of folk art, and
personal belongings. The documents and photographs
tell of Lenin's childhood, of his early revolutionary
activities, and his efforts to organize the Russian So-
cial-Democratic Labour Party. The exhibits illustrate the momentous events of October 1917, the armed
uprising, the overthrow of landlord and capitalist rule,
the heroism displayed in the Civil War, and the fight
against the interventionists, against hunger and destruction.

In a glass case in one of the halls is Lenin's modest overcoat, familiar to all from his photographs. It has a hole made by a bullet, which wounded Lenin when a villainous attempt was made on his life in 1918...

Numerous exhibits show how the Communist Party carried out Lenin's behests after his death.

A collection of objects of folk art—carpets, embroideries, carvings in bone and wood, drawings and paintings devoted to Lenin—is on display in several halls. It also includes professional works—paintings and sculptures dedicated to the great leader.

In a special hall, under lowered flags upon a pedestal are post-mortem moulds of Lenin's face and hands.

The museum was founded on May 15, 1936. In twenty years it was visited by 15,000,000 people.

The building occupied by the museum was built in 1892 by D. Chichagov in imitation of the ancient Russian style. Before the Revolution it was the City Duma, and in 1917 a refuge of counter-revolutionary elements of the Moscow bourgeoisie. Bitter battles ensued for its possession. Revolution Square was renamed from Voskresenskaya to

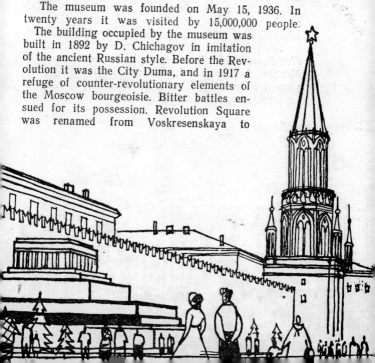

commemorate these battles. The square was an important commercial centre crossed from east to west by the Neglinka River. On the south side was the Kitai-Gorod wall, which merged with the Kremlin wall. The wall cut off Voskresenskaya Square from Red Square, and the two communicated by the Voskresenskiye Gate, from which a bridge was built in Boris Godunov's[4] day over the Neglinka to what is now Gorky Street. Later, when the Neglinka was enclosed in an underground conduit, the bridge was removed. The gates, however, were preserved until 1934.

Next to the Lenin Museum is a surface vestibule of the Metro, and opposite the latter, a delightful garden with a fountain by I. Vitali, the famous sculptor (1835). On the east side of the square is *Hotel Metropole*, whose front, opening upon Teatralny Lane, is adorned with a large majolika view by M. A. Vrubel.

The garden links Revolution Square with *Sverdlov Square* which is one of the handsomest squares in Moscow. In the past it was called Teatralnaya; its present name dates from 1921, when the square was renamed to commemorate Y. M. Sverdlov,[9] Chairman

metro

of the All-Russian Central Executive Committee of Soviets of Workers' and Soldiers' Deputies. The square acquired its present contours after Moscow was raised from the ashes of the 1812 fire. The Neglinka River, which had before run across the square, was then enclosed in an underground conduit. A quadrangle was fenced off in the middle of the square for army parades.

The building of the *Bolshoi Theatre*, designed by O. Bove and A. Mikhailov, was completed in 1824. In March 1853 the theatre was destroyed in a fire which lasted a whole week. Only the outer walls and the frontage survived. It was rebuilt in 1856.

The Bolshoi Theatre traces its history back to March 28, 1776, when a regular Russian professional musical theatre was first founded in Moscow.

In the early 19th century the Moscow musical opera and ballet company was placed under the management of the Administration of Imperial Theatres. This solved the theatre's financial problems to some extent, but committed its repertoire to the tastes of the upper crust of Russian society.

Ever since the middle of the 19th century, after the Moscow première (1842) of Glinka's *Ivan Susanin*, Bolshoi Theatre has been closely associated with the development of classical Russian opera and ballet music. At different times in its history, the theatre featured operas and ballets by Glinka and Dargomizhsky, Serov and Chaikovsky, Borodin and Musorgsky. The Bolshoi has reared a constellation of immortal Russian singers, such as Chaliapin, Sobinov, and Nezhdanova, who were associated with the theatre at the turn of the century. The Bolshoi's ballet company, along with that of the Petersburg theatre, have made Russian ballet known throughout the world.

The works of Western composers were prominently featured in the Bolshoi's repertoire. Classical operas by Mozart and Rossini, Auber and Wagner, Verdi and Gounod were often presented on its stage.

The Socialist Revolution helped to preserve for the people, and to develop, the distinctive art of this, Russia's greatest, opera house. In 1921, at Lenin's suggestion, the Bolshoi was titled an academic theatre. In 1937 it was decorated with the Order of Lenin for its outstanding contribution to Soviet music and the stage.

Most of its present-day singers are fledgelings of the Soviet school of music. A. Pirog'ov, M. Reisen, M. Mikhailov, I. Kozlovsky, S. Lemeshev, M. Maksakova, V. Davidova, G. Zhukovskaya, N. Shpiller, Y. Kruglikova, and P. Shumskaya are well known to Soviet theatre-goers and radio listeners. There are many gifted and rising young singers among the Bolshoi's interpreters. The Bolshoi also has an excellent choir and a first-class orchestra.

The Bolshoi's ballet is world famous. It has many striking performers, such as Galina Ulanova, Olga Lepeshinskaya, Maya Plisetskaya, Raisa Struchkova, Yury Kondratov, Yury Zhdanov, Georgy Farmanyants,

Koren, and many, many others. Furthermore, it has many young talents, reared by the Bolshoi Theatre's own school of choreography.

The Bolshoi Theatre company has more than a hundred opera soloists, a choir of 200, and more than 250 ballet dancers. Its orchestra comprises 250 musicians.

The present-day Bolshoi is a complex organism. To say nothing of its diverse electrical and mechanical equipment, without which modern productions with their lighting effects, etc., are unthinkable, the Bolshoi has another 24 auxiliary shops employing more than 500 people of different professions—expert shoemakers manufacturing ballet shoes; costumers and scenists who know how to lend the plainest materials an appearance of splendour; and the printers of its own printing-plant which puts out programmes, posters and the Bolshoi's newspaper, *Sovietsky Artist*. The five-tiered auditorium seats upwards of 2,000, and the capacity of the stage is just about as great, its size being almost equal to that of the auditorium. The audito-

rium is 25 metres long, 26 metres wide, and 21 metres high. The stage is 23.5 metres deep and 26 metres wide.

The theatre has its own museum, founded in 1921, which collects, arranges and studies materials relating to the history of the theatre.

On the right of the Bolshoi is the second-oldest theatre in the country, the *Maly Theatre*, founded in 1824. The Maly is the cradle of Russian realistic drama and the national school of acting. It has always been a vehicle of the most progressive ideas of the day. Such great Russian classics as Gogol,[15] Ostrovsky,[16] Turgenev[17] and Lev Tolstoi[18] worked on their plays in close collaboration with its producers and company. Several generations of Russian progressive intellectuals were brought up on the pick of the Russian and foreign plays produced on the Maly stage. "It is difficult to assess, record and imagine in terms of hard facts the profound spiritual influence which the Maly Theatre exercised, and continues to exercise," wrote Maxim Gorky.[19] "Together with Moscow University it plays a major, outstanding role in the history of the intellectual development of Russian society, and the future historian of the Maly Theatre will doubtlessly testify that it fulfilled its mission irreproachably."

The Revolution brought about what the Maly's foremost associates had dreamed of for many decades: the theatre's auditorium was flung open to the people. At present, the Maly Theatre devotes a substantial place in its repertoire to the works of Russian and foreign classics. At the same time, the theatre has staged several dozen modern plays by Soviet authors.

In 1929, a statue of *A. N. Ostrovsky*,[16] whose name is associated with an entire era in the Maly's history, was erected at its entrance. Ostrovsky's plays exposing the "realm of darkness" of feudal and merchant Russia, contributed to Maly's social importance and to the development of social thinking among the foremost intellectuals. The statue, by N. A. Andreyev, is a realistic portrait of the great Russian dramatist.

The Maly Theatre building has been repeatedly reconstructed in its more than a hundred years, but all piecemeal alterations failed to embellish it. It was only in 1947 that it was substantially enlarged, improved and equipped with up-to-date requisites. Its auditorium now has a seating capacity of 1,086.

On the corner of Petrovka Street, between the Bolshoi and Maly theatres, is the *Central Department Store*—one of the capital's largest emporiums.

On the left the Bolshoi neighbours the *Central Children's Theatre*, which enjoys tremendous popularity among juvenile theatre-goers. Pre-revolutionary Russia had no theatres for children. Now such theatres operate in most of regional cities.

Sverdlov Square communicates with Gorky Street by a short but busy thoroughfare known as *Okhotny Ryad*. At the close of the 19th century Okhotny Ryad was a quarter of food shops and groceries. The shops and open-air stalls carried on a brisk trade in meat,

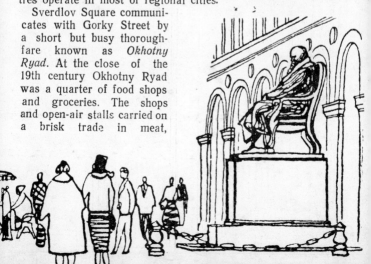

fish, fowl, vegetables and fruits. There were tea-shops, billiard parlours and restaurants. The middle of the street was occupied by a church, and next to that was a cab stand, horse-drawn vehicles being the principal means of city travel at that time. Downcast horses inertly chewed oats, while their masters, garbed in clumsy wide kaftans reaching down to their heels, and girdled with wide waistbands, loudly offered their services to passers-by. Tram-cars clamoured noisily for the right of way. An unholy racket filled the air. And in the backyards of the shops butchers slaughtered fowl and cattle in defiance of all sanitary regulations.

In the thirties Okhotny Ryad was one of the first to undergo a radical reconstruction. The shops, tea-houses and the church were torn down. Just two old buildings were spared—one on the corner of Pushkin Street, now known as *Dom Soyuzov* (House of Trade Unions), and the other on the opposite corner, which now houses the three-dimensional cinema.

Dom Soyuzov was built in the eighteen eighties by Matvei Kazakov[6] for Field Marshal Prince Dolgoruky. But the Dolgorukys sold it to the Club of Nobility as a site for its

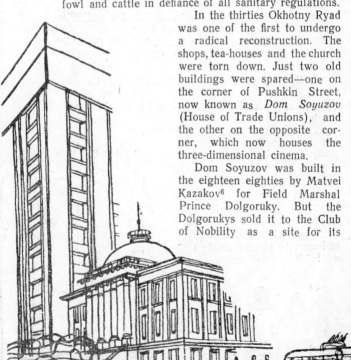

gala balls and gatherings. Dom Soyuzov is known for its *Kolonny Zal* (Hall of Columns). Stately rows of columns run majestically along the walls of the hall, exquisite chandeliers shedding a soft light upon the red velvet of its chairs. Today the Hall of Columns is used for city Party gatherings, memorial meetings, congresses and conferences of government, trade-union and public bodies. It is also one of the capital's major concert halls.

The rest of the block, from Dom Soyuzov to Gorky Street, is occupied by the *U.S.S.R. Council of Ministers* building, by A. Y. Langman, built in 1935. In the same year, *Moskva Hotel*, by Academician Shchusev, went up on the opposite side of the street, occupying most of the block. The hotel has 492 suites, and this year construction work will begin on its second section, which will have 600 suites.

Full-grown lime-trees were planted on both sides of Okhotny Ryad in 1947. The 60-metre roadway has to cope with extremely heavy traffic.

The new thoroughfare involved a radical reconstruction of all adjacent blocks. Part of Gorky Street and houses on the left side of Mokhovaya Street up to Herzen Street, and houses along the street which led from the History Museum to the Manège, had to be removed lock, stock and barrel to open up the façade of Moskva Hotel and extend the access to Okhotny Ryad. The spacious Manège Square is a result of all this.

S trange as it may seem, Manège Square in the
very heart of ancient Moscow is one of the newest
squares in the city. It was laid out in the early
thirties in connection with the city reconstruction project. After all dwelling-houses were torn down on the
site now occupied by the square, an open space remained, bordered on all sides by buildings of distinction.

On the south side, for instance, is the building of
the *History Museum*, built by Sherwood in 1881 in imitation of the ancient Russian style. The magnificent
Alexandrovsky Garden stretches along the foot of the
Kremlin wall. Under it, enclosed in subterranean conduits, runs the Neglinka. On the west side is the *Manège*, designed by A. Betancour, and built in 1817. It
has a remarkable flat 45-metre timber canopy of raft-
ers and tie-beams, supported by the outer walls alone,
without a single intervening stanchion, a regular architectural feat in its day. The Manège was used as
a riding-school for officers, and was frequently the
site of exhibitions and charity balls.

On the north side, the square is bordered by the classical edifice of *Moscow State University*, built in 1793 by Matvei Kazakov.[6] After the 1812 fire Architect Gilardi restored the building in keeping with its original design, but succeeded in adding somewhat to its grandeur. Against the setting of this classical architectural ensemble, nearer the front wings, stand the statues by Andreyev of Herzen[20] and Ogaryov,[21] the foremost representatives of progressive Russian thought in the eighteen forties, fifties and sixties. The monuments were unveiled in 1922.

The second building of the University was erected in 1836 at 11, Mokhovaya Street. The semi-circle of columns, which terminates the right wing of the second building (Architect Tyurin) harmonizes with the semi-circle of the old building's annex, joining them in a single ensemble. Curiously, the usage of differentiating the buildings as "old" and "new" persists to this day, although the really new building of the University is on the Lenin Hills.

Both University buildings, and several other blocks behind them, are occupied by humanistic departments, such as the philosophical, historical, philological, economic, and the departments of law and journalism.

Between the "old" University building and a dwelling-house built in 1934 (by Zholtovsky) is the Geological Prospecting Institute. In its day the house by

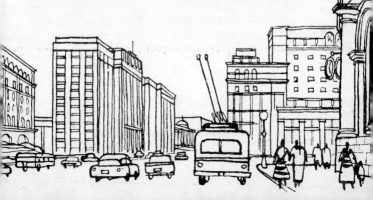

Zholtovsky was the cause of considerable controversy. In the search for new architectural forms many architects often ignored classical schemes, which they regarded as outdated, and the appearance of some of their buildings was, therefore, often severe, primitive and uninviting. Zholtovsky, on the other hand, made bold with classical architectural forms.

The corner where Manège Square merges with Gorky Street is occupied by *Hotel National*.

On the east side of Manège Square is *Moskva Hotel*, which faces the square with its imposing four-storey portico.

The spacious, newly built Manège Square, which adjoins the new Okhotny Ryad, is in harmony with the appearance of the city centre, formed by Red Square, Dzerzhinsky Square, Sverdlov Square and Revolution Square.

Manège Square, in a manner of speaking, is the mouth of the capital's main three-kilometre artery—*Gorky Street*—whose reconstruction was completed before the outbreak of war in 1941. Between *Hotel Na-*

tional and Sovietskaya Square only a single old block, including the *Yermolova Drama Theatre*, has been preserved on the left side of the street before the *Central Telegraph Office,* by I. I. Rerberg, built in 1930. Houses Nos. 9 and 11, which follow the Telegraph Office, were completed in 1949. The entire right side of the street has been built anew after a design by Architect Mordvinov. The new housing development has been pushed back somewhat, widening the thoroughfare from its former 17 to 60 metres. The ground floors are occupied by various shops. In one of the houses in the beginning of the street, for instance, is a large store of souvenirs and presents.

The block between Okhothy Ryad and Khudozhestvenny Teatr Lane is occupied by a single housing project cut by an archway issuing into Georgievsky Lane. In Khudozhestvenny Teatr Lane is the *Moscow Art Theatre*, treasure-trove of the Russian national drama.

The Art Theatre was founded in 1898 by K. S. Stanislavsky[22] and V. I. Nemirovich-Danchenko,[23] and has travelled an arduous, eminently important road as the pioneer of new methods of stagecraft, embodying a profound understanding of reality and a lofty sense of social duty. The progressive principles of the Art Theatre, introduced by Stanislavsky, have had a marked influence upon the practices of Soviet and advanced foreign theatres. The Art Theatre preserves and develops the best traditions of Stanislavsky and Nemirovich-Danchenko. The theatre has its own experimental scenic workshops, its own school of stagecraft, and its own museum.

Two blocks away along Gorky Street is *Sovietskaya Square*. In the middle is a statue of *Yury Dolgoruky*,[2] the founder of Moscow. The bronze equestrian figure in a **coat** of mail is mounted on a rectangular pedestal of dark grey polished granite adorned with ancient Russian ornaments. The monument was laid in 1947 to commemorate Moscow's 800th anniversary, and unveiled on June 6, 1954.

Opposite the statue is the *Moscow City Soviet of Working People's Deputies.* This handsome edifice was built in 1782 by Kazakov[6] for the Governor-General of Moscow. The house was relatively small, and in 1930 a subsidiary building was erected at its back in an entirely different style. In 1946 Architect Chechulin moved back the main edifice 11 metres, added two more storeys to it, and built solid walls to connect it with the subsidiary building. As a result, the two made up a single massive block, much like the original edifice in style and form. The new edifice has an artistically ornamented enclosure with two eleven-metre ironwork gates and two similar wickets, mounted upon white-stone columns and adorned with bronze embellishments.

Present-day Sovietskaya Square is a far cry from the empty lot where the Moscow Governor-General's guard set its sentries some 150 years ago. It was only after 1812, when reconstruction was in full swing following the big fire, that houses sprang up in this locality. On the square, where the

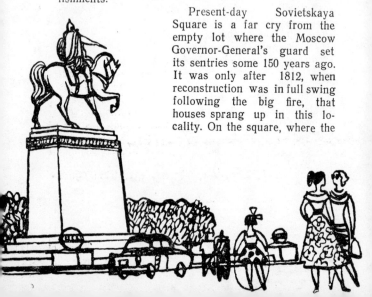

pleasure garden is today, a guard house and a fire-tower were built in 1823 for the police department and fire-brigade. In 1923, exactly one hundred years later, the structures were torn down.

A row of modern dwelling-houses, by Mordvinov, stretches from Sovietskaya Square along the left side of Gorky Street. The architect achieved an imposing, buoyant effect.

The frontage of the house adjoining the Moscow Soviet is cut by an archway opening upon *Stanislavsky Street*, formerly called Leontyevsky Lane, in which, in house No. 18, the Moscow Committee of the Communist Party was located the first few years after the Revolution. On September 25, 1919, counter-revolutionaries threw a bomb into its conference hall during a sitting. A memorial plaque of coloured granite has been mounted on the house in tribute to the victims.

In May 1904, when last visiting Moscow, A. P. Chekhov[24] resided in house No. 24 of the same lane. "I stay ... in Leontyevsky Lane (Katyk's house, where the great Chaliapin lives)," Chekhov wrote in one of his letters. House No. 6 was the long-time residence of People's Actor Stanislavsky.[22] The house is at present a museum, where exhibits are collected to illustrate the life's work of the gifted actor and stage director. Three

memorial rooms are maintained just the way they were during his lifetime. It was to perpetuate his memory that the thoroughfare was renamed.

After Stanislavsky's death Nemirovich-Danchenko continued to direct the Art Theatre. The counterpart of Stanislavsky Street on the opposite side of Gorky Street is named in his honour. The building of the former Kopp Hotel, in which A. S. Pushkin[25] resided on many occasions, still stands in *Nemirovich-Danchenko Street.* Here the poet was visited by the great Polish bard, Mickiewicz. In 1956 a plaque in high relief was mounted upon the wall of the house to commemorate the friendship of the two bards, on which Mickiewicz and Pushkin are portrayed at full height against the setting of the "Bronze Horseman"—the monument to Peter I,[1] to whom both poets dedicated inspired lines. The high relief is by Milberger, a young Polish sculptor, who attended Surikov Art Institute in Moscow.

On the left side of Gorky Street houses No. 15 and No. 17 have archways in their façades issuing into Bolshoi Gnezdnikovsky Lane. Here stands an old ten-storey house, the tallest building in pre-revolutionary Moscow. A view of the entire city opened from its flat roof. But the former "giant" is now lost among the new buildings around it.

The corner of house No. 17, occupied by the "Armenia" provision store, is topped by a large statue of a girl, arms spread wide in happy, carefree welcome to the rising sun. The walls inside the store are adorned with mosaics by Vartanyan, laid with several thousand stones—coloured smalt, jasper, malakhite and pink rhodonite.

On the other side of Gorky Street is "Gastronom" No. 1. In the eighteen twenties the building, which has been enirely re-built since then, housed the famous literary salon of Princess Zinaida Volkonskaya, at which Russia's most distinguished men of letters, and artists, Pushkin[25] among them, used to congregate.

The home-museum of Nikolai Ostrovsky, the Soviet writer, is in his former flat at house No. 14, Gorky Street. Among the exhibits are the manuscripts, documents, books, favourite belongings, portraits and photographs of the author of *How the Steel was Tempered* and *Born of the Storm*, the favourite books of young people.

Pushkin Square is widely known for the monument to the immortal poet. The statue, by Opekushin, was erected with funds subscribed by the population. It was unveiled in 1880 at the end of Tverskoi Boulevard. During the centennial of the death of Pushkin in 1937, the original lines of Pushkin's *Monument* were restored upon its granite pedestal instead of those altered by tsarist censors:

> *Word of my fame will sweep through mighty Russia*
> *And all its tongues will speak my name:*
> *The haughty Slav, and Finn, and the now savage*
> *Tungus, and Kalmik riders of the plain.*
> *And to the people long shall I be dear*
> *Because kind feelings did my lyre extoll,*
> *Invoking freedom in an age of fear,*
> *And mercy for the broken soul.*

At the same time former *Strastnaya Square* was renamed in tribute to the great poet.

Pushkin Square used to be called Strastnaya after the Strastnoi Women's Monastery, which occupied it since 1654. In the 18th century the square was the site of small shops, smithies, workshops, and a hay market. In the 19th century many mansions and dwelling-houses were built there, one of which, house No. 3 on the north side of the square, has

survived to this day. It belonged to Rimskaya-Korsakova, who entertained numerous distinguished guests, and notably Pushkin[25] and Griboyedov.[26] Some say that at her gatherings Griboyedov picked upon the classical prototypes of his immortal *Wit Works Woe.*

After the Revolution Strastnaya Square was reconstructed. A large grey building was erected in 1927 (alongside Rimskaya-Korsakova's house) occupied by the editorial offices, publishing house and printing plant of the *Izvestia*, the organ of the Presidium of the Supreme Soviet of the U.S.S.R. The Strastnoi Monastery and its adjoining structures were torn down in the thirties, and the square widened to its present size; in 1950, a garden was laid out on the former monastery grounds with fountains and granite parapets, and the Pushkin monument was transferred to the square from Tverskoi Boulevard. Fullgrown lime-trees were planted along the edge of the sidewalks.

The left side of Gorky Street, between Pushkin Square and Mayakovsky Square, was entirely rebuilt in the past fifteen years. The former English Club and the Ophthalmologic Hospital are the only two old-time buildings to survive. In the 18th century the English Club was a resort of the Moscow aristocracy. Today the building, and its new annexes, are occupied by the *Museum of the Revolution.*

The Museum, founded in 1924, is dedicated to the history of the Great October Socialist Revolution and Soviet society. Its exhibits are on display in eleven halls.

Next to the Museum is the *Stanislavsky Drama Theatre*, which evolved from an opera and drama studio directed by Stanislavsky,[22] who used it as an experimental laboratory for his stage system.

The Ophthalmologic Hospital, which formerly faced Gorky Street, was turned 90 degrees during the reconstruction and moved down Sadovskikh Lane, named after the famous family of Maly Theatre actors.

Some way down is *Mayakovsky Square* (of which more on page 75). On the corner of Gorky Street, on our right, is the *Central Puppet Theatre* directed by People's Actor Sergei Obraztsov, a truly unique and fascinating institution. The Soviet puppet theatre has gone a long way from the traditional old-time Punch-and-Judy show. Obraztsov evolved a puppet show all his own and gave it distinctive qualities of style and genre that distinguish it from the ordinary marionettes. Its highly popular repertoire includes topical and caustic satire and parody. The theatre's shows for children are equally enjoyed by grown-ups.

Beyond Mayakovsky Square new dwellings and office buildings rise along Gorky Street. They date back to the thirties and forties. In one of them (No. 43 on the left side of the street) is the *"House of Children's Books,"* which conducts research in the spheres of literary criticism, theory and history of children's books, and the interests and requirements of juvenile readers. There are two reading-rooms in the house for tiny tots and older children. The house also has a conference hall, where writers are introduced to their readers at lectures and literary gatherings. Diverse information concerning juvenile literature is available at the department of bibliography.

The set of buildings of the *Embassy of the Republic of Czechoslovakia*, a bright and interesting effort by a group of Czechoslovak and Soviet engineers, deserves mention. It is in Novo-Vasilyevskaya Street, which adjoins Gorky Street. The façades of the seven-storey Embassy building and two five-storey dwelling-houses, connected by a wall and large ironwork gates, open upon the street. In the courtyard is a pavilion hall intended for diplomatic receptions, and a third dwelling-house. The structures are girded by a flower garden, in the middle of which is a fountain. The frontage is finished in ceramics, wood, polished granite, and mosaic embellishments of coloured ceramic tiles. The interior is finished in artificial and natural marble, diverse wood species, and brocade. The ornamental designs draw upon Czech and Slovak folk themes. Czech workers and experts took part in the interior decorations. The set of buildings was completed late in 1955.

Gorky Street ends at the square before *Byelorussia Railway Station*, built in 1909. Trains leave the terminal for the western border of the Soviet Union. On the square is a picturesque flower garden with a *statue of Gorky*,[19] by Vera Mukhina, one of the leading Soviet sculptors, after a design by Ivan Shadr.

* * *

In the 16th century present-day Gorky Street was called Tverskaya, and was the main road from Moscow to the city of Tver (now Kalinin), Novgorod, and, later, to Petersburg (Leningrad). The street ended at what is now Mayakovsky Square. Farther on were peasant huts and yards, vegetable gardens and fields. These made up the village of the coachmen plying this busy highway. The village was turned to ashes in the fire of 1773, and small brick dwellings were later built on its site for the coachmen. A series of coachmen's streets (*Yamskie,* from *yamshchik,* the Russian for coachman), known to this day as Tverskiye-Yamskiye, took shape in the district, in which some of the houses still stand.

After railways were introduced in the 19th century the coachmen's quarter fell into disrepair. Tverskaya Street was extended to Byelorussia Station. New dwelling-houses, shops, taverns and boarding-houses appeared. Horse-drawn tram-cars, which later gave way to electrically driven vehicles, began to run here in 1872. Yet a mere hundred and fifty years ago the Tverskaya turnpike stood on the site of the square in front of Byelorussia Station, where a soldier veteran checked the travelling papers of persons entering the city.

Pushkin,[25] who had repeatedly entered Moscow by the Tverskaya turnpike, left a brilliant description of Tverskaya Street of the eighteen twenties.

> *Now Peter's fort, farewell, attesting*
> *Those fallen glories! White show*
> *The barrier-pillars; now, unresting,*
> *Along Tverskaya let us go.*
> *The coach along the ruts is dashing;*
> *Stalls, countrywomen, by are flashing:*
> *Watchboxes, children at their play,*
> *Convent and palace, lamp and sleigh,*
> *Bukharian, merchant, Cossack, peasant;*
> *Huts, drugstores, boulevards, and towers,*
> *And gardens both for fruit and flowers;*
> *Shops telling what's the mode at present;*
> *Balconies, lions topping gates;*
> *And daws, on every cross, in spates.*

(Yevgeny Onegin, Ch. 7, XXXVII)

Beyond Byelorussia Station and the viaduct over the railway tracks begins *Leningrad Highway*—a superb motor-road with fine green medial strips.

On its right is the *2nd Watch Factory* and the *"Java"* Tobacco Factory, and a little farther, *Pravda Street* branches away in which is the country's largest *Pravda Printing Plant*, built in 1935. It prints the *Pravda, Sovietskaya Rossiya,*

Komsomolskaya Pravda, and the journals *Kommunist, Ogonyok, Rabotnitsa, Krestyanka, Krokodil, Oktyabr, Znamya,* etc.

On the left side of Leningrad Highway are the red buildings of the *Bolshevik Confectionery,* and on the right, the fine building of *Sovietskaya Hotel.* It is adjoined by *Dom Kino* (Cinema Centre), the club of the motion picture industry.

On the opposite side of the highway is the gateway of a tree-shaded alley leading to the grandstands of the *Moscow Race Course.* The gates are adorned with bronze replicas of the famous man-and-horse statues by Klodt, mounted on Anichkov Bridge in Leningrad.

In the vicinity, separated from the Race Course by Begovaya Street, is the *Stadium of Young Pioneers.* Here junior sportsmen are offered all possible facilities, such as a Palace of Physical Culture, sports grounds, a football field, a velodrome, and a roofed year-round skating-rink with artificial ice.

Beyond the stadium is the *Botkin Hospital,* one of the biggest in the capital.

The large area to the north-west was formerly a vast empty lot—the Khodinskoye Field. It was a summer camping ground of the Moscow garrison, its drill ground and shooting range. Besides, it was also the site of the Moscow Aeronautics Society's airfield.

In 1896 coronation festivities were held on Khodinskoye Field to mark the accession of the last Russian tsar, Nicholas II. Striving to create a semblance of popular enthusiasm, the Moscow Governor-General scheduled a celebration, promising presents and free entertainment. Huge crowds poured on to the field. The sponsors, meanwhile, had not taken even elementary steps to maintain law and order. The narrow passages between show-booths and marquees were crowded to suffocation. The day was hot. People suffered heat strokes and fell, and were trampled to death. Nearly 2,000 died that day at the royal "festivities." The Khodinskoye calamity is written into the history of tsarist autocracy as one of the darkest pages of Nicholas's reign. Indignation swept Russia as word spread of the tsar's "benefaction" at Khodinskoye Field. The word "Khodinka" has since become a by-word.

On the right side of Leningrad Highway, in the heart of what once was the verdant Petrovsky Park, is the *Dynamo Stadium*, built in 1928. Prior to the completion of the stadium in Luzhniki it was the capital's chief sports arena with a seating capacity of 80,000 covering an area of 45 hectares (110 acres).

Near the stadium is *Petrovsky Palace*, built by Matvei Kazakov in the late 18th century. The royal family used to stop at the palace en route from Petersburg, before entering Moscow in state. Napoleon, frightened by the huge Moscow fire, sought refuge in the palace in 1812. It was this that Pushkin[25] had in mind in his lines: "Now Peter's fort, farewell, attesting those fallen glories!"
At present the

building belongs to the *Zhukovsky*[27] *Air Academy,* and a bust of Zhukovsky, the great scientist in aeronautics, is installed before the main entrance.

Many large structures have gone up in recent years beyond the palace, in the vicinity of Sokol Settlement. More building is in progress today. The *Indoor Swimming Pool of the Central Sports Club of the Ministry of Defence,* completed in 1955 (Leningrad Highway, 55-a, near Aeroport Metro Station), merits the visitor's attention. The pool covers an area of 1,000 sq. metres (1,200 sq. yards). Its eight tracks are adapted for all world championship swimming events, since it conforms to the international swimming rules. It is also equipped with diving platforms and spring-boards. The pool is the scene of frequent water-polo contests. Showers, training halls, baths and massage rooms are available. The grandstands have a seating capacity of 2,000.

Somewhat farther from the forking, *Volokolamsk Highway* branches away to the left, leading to the woods of *Pokrovskoye Streshnevo,* while 12 kilometres (8 miles) away along Leningrad Highway is the *"Khimki" River-Port* on the Moscow Canal.

We leave the highway and drive up to the river-port by the main park alley. The park is a dense grove, though less than twenty years old. It was laid when construction work at the port was still in progress. The outer appearance of the port building with its softly rounded corners and a tall tower is

72

faintly suggestive of a ship at anchor. Sculptures and murals are widely applied in the interior decorations. The shine of marble walls and ornate mural embellishments give it an air of splendour.

Returning up Leningrad Highway, we turn right at Marina Raskova Square into Novo-Peschanaya Street, an entirely new residential quarter. Numerous dwellings have gone up on the Peschanaya and Novo-Peschanaya streets and the streets of *Bolshoye Oktyabrskoye Field* in the past ten years. The houses were built at a rapid pace, and are distinguished by their pleasing, simple, and modest lines. The district housing development may rightly be called progressive, because prefabricated section assembly methods were first applied in it.

The 7th block of Novo-Peschanaya Street was an empty lot when builders first came there a mere two years ago. Its houses were built from prefabricated sections produced at various plants of the building industry. Foundation blocks, pillars, sections of roofs and walls arrived at the construction site ready for assembly. Pioneers of large-section frameless building are busy on the 4th Street of Bolshoye Oktyabrskoye Field, erecting a storey every 12 days.

After driving through the Peschanaya, Novo-Peschanaya and the 6th Street of the Bolshoye Oktyabrskoye Field, we come to *Khoroshevskoye Highway*, where another community of new dwellings comes to view. This housing development was begun before the war in 1941, somewhat earlier than the Peschaniye project.

By Khoroshevskoye Highway we come to Begovaya Street, which has also been completely reconstructed in recent years. Only a few small cottages remind us of the old Begovaya of the twenties and thirties. As we approach Leningrad Highway the new Race Course building, by Zholtovsky, comes to view on the right, completed in 1955. On the left is the handsome enclosure of the Stadium of Young Pioneers, which we round to turn into Leningrad Highway and return to the centre of the city.

MAYAKOVSKY SQUARE—VOSSTANIYE SQUARE—SMOLENSKAYA SQUARE—KRIMSKY BRIDGE—BOLSHAYA KALUZHSKAYA ST.—LENIN HILLS—UNIVERSITY—KALUZHSKAYA SQUARE—BOLSHAYA YAKIMANKA ST.— SOFIISKAYA EMBANKMENT—RED SQUARE

Mayakovsky Square is situated on the crossing of the city's main arteries—Gorky Street and Sadovoye Circle. The square bears the name of Vladimir Mayakovsky,[28] the leading poet of the Soviet epoch, who died in 1930. A statue of him, on which work is now in progress, will be erected here.

Mayakovsky Square occupies a site in the former Zemlyanoi Gorod, on Zemlyanoi Val—old Moscow's fourth line of defence (see page 11). In 1812 Zemlyanoi Gorod was razed to the ground, and was rebuilt in later years. The earthen embankment was demolished, and the moat filled in. A wide street took shape along former Zemlyanoi Val in the 19th century, with predominantly small dwelling-houses, little gardens before them, and with boulevards and gardens in the intervening squares. An incomplete circle of Sadovaya streets evolved, sections of which eventually adopted the names of either the adjacent square or the nearest radial street, as, for example, Sadovo-Kudrinskaya Street, Sadovo-Karetnaya Street, etc.

After 1935 the Sadovoye Circle underwent a radical reconstruction. The tramway was torn up. Numerous new dwelling-houses rose on both sides of the resultant modern thoroughfare.

Present-day Mayakovsky Square is a square of theatres. Mention has already been made of Obraztsov's Puppet Theatre (see page 66). On the south side of the square is *Chaikovsky*[29] *Concert Hall* with an impressive portico and a picturesque windowless wall. Next to it is the *Light Opera Theatre*, followed by *Aquarium Garden*, now the construction site of the new Mossoviet Theatre building, and opposite it, across the square, is the *Variety Theatre* and the *Moskva Cinema*.

Mayakovsky Square is a busy intersection. A two-way underground tunnel for vehicles and two underground passages for pedestrians are planned to cross Gorky Street along Sadovoye Circle. The passages will communicate with the Mayakovsky Metro Station. Traffic at several levels will make for greater safety and eliminate traffic jams.

Bolshaya Sadovaya Street, which has undergone great changes in the past twenty years, runs southwest from Mayakovsky Square. The street begins with the new *Peking Hotel* building on the right, and the austere administrative office building (No. 8a) on the left.

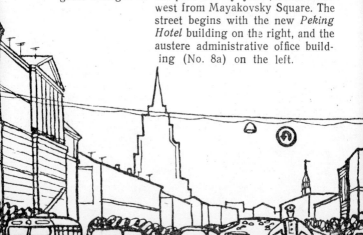

Bolshaya Sado- vaya merges with *Sadovo-Kudrinskaya Street*, in which the egg-shaped silver cupola of the *Planetarium* is the first to attract attention. The Moscow Planetarium was opened in 1929, and its popular lec-  tures and demonstrations of celestial bodies have made it a centre of attraction to both Muscovites and out-of-town visitors. At present the Planetarium is being re-equipped with improved apparatus, and will undergo a reconstruction. Its new building will house the Meteoritic Museum of the Academy of Sciences, an exhibition of the Structure of the Universe, special premises for studies in astronomy and geography, and a public astronomical observatory. Two 18-metre towers will grace the main entrance.

On the left side of the street, in house No. 6, is the *Chekhov*[24] *Museum*. The house was occupied by the writer in 1886-90. The exhibits include his personal belongings, some manuscripts and portraits.

Farther on is *Vosstaniye Square*, whose present appearance evolved in the past decade. It has been greatly extended after adjacent old dwelling-houses were torn down. A 22-storey edifice with 450 flats now rises in their stead. In the lower stories of the building is Moscow's largest "Gastronom." A picture house and a café operate in the sub-base. A flower garden has been laid out before the edifice.

77

On the north-east side of the square, to the right of the 22-storey building, is an old structure built in 1785 by Kazakov[6] and re-built after the 1812 fire by Gilardi. Its laconic monumental forms, and the combination of smooth walls with a gala portico, are typical of Russian early 19th century classicism. It was an alms-house for widows, officials and retired officers, and was known as "Widows' Home." At present it houses the *Central Graduate Medical Institute* and other institutions of the Public Health Ministry. Under the Reconstruction Plan the "Widows' Home" will be eventually moved back to the grounds of the Zoo, and will occupy a site facing Barrikadnaya and Kachalov streets. This will open a wide, straight thoroughfare from the centre to Krasnopresnenskaya Zastava and Zvenigorod Highway.

Vosstaniye Square and the adjoining district of *Krasnaya Presnya* have gone down in history as the site of heroic battles between the Russian proletariat and tsarist troops sent in December 1905 to crush the Moscow armed uprising.

A small, unimpressive-looking old house on the south-eastern side of the square bears a memorial plaque which identifies it as the residence of Pyotr Chaikovsky,[29] the celebrated Russian composer. His name has also been given to the adjoining block of Sadovoye Circle, which brings us to Smolenskaya Square. The towering multi-storey building erected in the square in 1952 catches the eye from afar. The building's volume is 400,000 cu. metres, and it is 170 metres high. It houses the *Foreign Ministry* and the *Ministry of Foreign Trade*.

Farther on is *Zubovskaya Square*. It perpetuates the name of Zubovskiye Gate, which in the 17th century afforded exit from the city by Staraya Smolenskaya Road to Lithuania. A fine view of Krimsky Bridge opens from the square. But before approaching the bridge let us examine the right side of the street, which presents a curious mixture of architectural styles. The corner house, built early in the century, is an effort to return to Russian "Empire" architectural forms (early 19th century), and somewhat farther on is the house of the former royal Court Administration (No. 27), an example of the true "Empire" style—with abstract and clearcut forms and all the embellishments typical of the style. It is adjoined by a small, provincial-type single-storey wooden house with five windows and a mezzanine floor. Another toy-like house of its kind follows, and the façade of a modern 6-storey building (No. 15) hides from view a typical mansion of the early 19th century, which had formerly stood in the heart of a large courtyard, and had a verandah at the back, opening upon a spacious garden. This mingling of styles and epochs is typical of the outskirts of old-time Moscow.

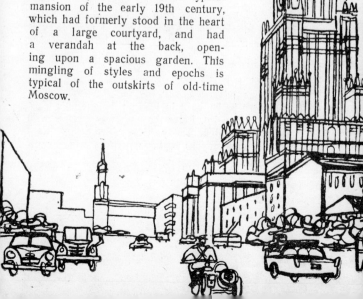

Near Krimsky Bridge, on the left side of Krimskaya Square, are haughty structures—the food depots—designed by Stasov, the outstanding Russian architect, and completed in the eighteen thirties. In 1917 stubborn fighting, which lasted several days, ensued for possession of the depots between the revolutionary Red Guard and armed counter-revolutionary elements.

On the right side is the surface vestibule of a Metro station, and in the distance, above the green of the trees, is a glimpse of the ancient *Church of St. Nicholas in Khamovniki** (1682).

Krimsky Bridge was built in 1936-38 by Architect Vlasov and Engineer Konstantinov. Its roadway is suspended from huge vertical pylons by means of a long, continuous ribbon of steel bars and supports. It is 38.5 metres wide.

Beyond Krimsky Bridge, along the bank of the Moskva, sprawls *Gorky*[19] *Recreation Park*, one of the first modern parks, built in 1928 on the site of a large empty suburban lot. Later the park was merged with Neskuchny Garden. Today Gorky Recreation Park covers an area of 110 hectares, half of which com-

---

* *Khamovniki* is old Russian for, weavers, whose quarter it was in the dim past.

prises its regular part, with all kinds of park facilities—amusement devices, a picture house, libraries, open-air stages, exhibition halls, cafés, restaurants, etc. Attractive tree-shaded promenades, flower-beds, ponds, and a boat-house and landing-stage on the river bank, complete the picture. The alleys, the riverside and most of the open spaces are in winter turned into a skating-rink.

Beyond the open-air Green Theatre the outlines of the regular park end abruptly, giving way to a hilly plateau cut by numerous ravines and miniature ponds. This is the former site of the ancient *Neskuchny Garden*, in which giant old oaks, century-old limes, willows and elms, spread their boughs to this day. Footpaths lead away to the Lenin Hills, past green glades dotted with field flowers.

Once over Krimsky Bridge, we enter *Zamoskvorechye*, one of Moscow's oldest districts. Until recently it had distinctive features all its own, developed down the years.

The meadowland on the right bank of the Moskva, upon which Zamoskvorechye arose, was in the dim past arable land belonging to the princely court. It was crossed by a lively south-bound trade route to the Crimean and Astrakhan Tatars, to Persia and Central Asia. Zamoskvorechye, however, was vulnerable to hostile raids, and particularly raids by the nomad-

ic Mongol Tatars. For this reason the two monasteries —Danilov, founded in 1272, and Donskoi, founded in 1592—on the southern outskirt of Zamoskvorechye, were veritable strongholds.

In the 16th century *streltsi* settled in Zamoskvorechye, forming their own *streltsi* community, with vegetable gardens and fields.

Nearer the bank, opposite the Kremlin, were communities of court retainers—minters, farmers, gardeners, tanners, interpreters, coopers, etc.

As Moscow expanded and its commerce developed, and the Golden Horde grew less aggressive, Zamoskvorechye became a residential quarter of merchants. In the 18th and 19th centuries Moscow merchants developed into a powerful commercial and financial body and the merchants of Zamoskvorechye were their most typical representatives. They were a class of their own, with peculiar, conservative traditions, customs and morals.

The Moscow merchant is vividly depicted in Russian literature, particularly in the plays of Alexander Ostrovsky.[16] The ways of Zamoskvorechye merchants were also strikingly portrayed in canvases by Fedotov, Perov and Pryanishnikov.

Since the Revolution Zamoskvorechye has considerably changed. The change leaps to the eye as we

drive from Oktyabrskaya (Kaluzhskaya) Square to Moscow University. This section of Zamoskvorechye, it should be noted, was in the past a distant city outskirt. On the right side, in the woodland stretching along the bank of the Moskva, were the suburban villas and summerhouses of the wealthy. In the mid-19th century the lots were acquired by the royal Court Administration and turned into Neskuchny Garden. At present the grounds have become part of Gorky Recreation Park. On the left side were the small wooden dwellings of townsmen and artisans, and beyond them the vegetable gardens of the Danilov and Donskoi monasteries.

In 1796-1801 the Golitsin Hospital, one of the finest edifices by Kazakov,[6] was erected on the right. It still stands (and is now part of the set of buildings comprising the *Pervaya Gradskaya Hospital*).

The reconstruction of *Bolshaya Kaluzhskaya Street* was launched in 1939. Twelve multi-storey buildings were erected in less than 18 months. But unlike the houses in Gorky Street, they stand at intervals, with the intervening greenery of parks and gardens affording a pleasing respite to the eye. The wide, straight and comfortable thoroughfare with its new houses against a setting of dense foliage, linked with the centre of the city by Metro, trolley-bus and bus routes, was one of the first major reconstruction projects to be completed. Subsequently, new houses went up on the left side of the street. Such leading Soviet architects as Mordvinov, Golts and Chechulin collaborated in the reconstruction of Bolshaya Kaluzhskaya Street.

The thoroughfare opens with a building (No. 6) housing three major institutions of higher learning: the *Oil Institute*, the *Mining Institute* and the *Steel Institute*.

Farther on, in a handsome palace (No. 16) built in 1756 by Prokofy Demidov, the wealthy industrialist, is the *Presidium of the U.S.S.R. Academy of Sciences*. In one of its annexes is the world-known *Mineralogical Museum of the Academy of Sciences*, which contains highly valuable and rare collections of minerals.

Along Bolshaya Kaluzhskaya Street and its continuation, known as Vorobyovskoye Highway, are research institutes of the Academy of Sciences, such as the mathematical and electrical institutes, and the institutes of mineral fuels, biology, physical chemistry, biochemistry, microbiology and others.

Bolshaya Kaluzhskaya Street ends at the viaduct of the Okruzhnaya Railway, beyond which begins Vorobyovskoye Highway, running across a wooded district sprawling on the slopes of the Lenin Hills, formerly

called Vorobyovo Hills after the village that stood there in the recent past. The Lenin Hills is a favourite recreation resort. A splendid wood, the wide expanse of river, and a breath-taking view of Moscow from the eminences, make it a centre of attraction. In winter ski jumping competitions are held on its slopes.

The Lenin Hills are the site of the new buildings of *Moscow University*, which have changed the appearance of the entire locality beyond recognition.

At the approaches to the University is the luxuriant greenery of newly planted trees, lawns and flower-beds. Parks and gardens cover an area of 100 hectares around the University. More than 50,000 trees, about 500,000 bushes and upwards of 1,000,000 different flowers were planted there. The trees and bushes are of diverse species, including species earlier unknown in Moscow and its environs. Flowers bloom hereabouts from early spring to late autumn in colourful succession. A sprawling green parterre leads to the University building from Vorobyovskoye Highway. Near the edifice is an artificial lakelet, adorned with granite busts of distinguished Russian scientists—Lomonosov,[30] Lobachevsky,[31] Herzen,[20] Chernyshevsky,[32] Mendeleyev,[33] Popov,[34] Timiryazev,[35] Michurin,[36] Zhukovsky,[27] Pavlov,[37] Dokuchayev,[33] and Chebyshev.[39]

The Government decision to build the new University premises on the Lenin Hills was made public on March 15, 1948, and on September 1, 1953, its doors were flung open to students.

The new University premises are a set of 37 distinct structures—an integral architectural ensemble of buildings, two, three, six, nine, twelve and eighteen storeys high, symmetrically arranged round the main 32-storey edifice topped by a tall spire. The main edifice is about 240 metres high. Add the eighty metres to which the Lenin Hills, the highest point of the city, rise here above the level of the Moskva River, and you will readily see how far away the University is visible on a clear day.

A wide granite stairway leads up to the main entrance. Eight 14-metre columns of pink marble comprise the portico, flanked on both sides by bronze statues by People's Artist Mukhina. Above the columns is a large bas-relief of many figures by Motovilov, titled "Creators." The portico is crowned with a bronze bas-relief of the Order of Lenin, with which Moscow University has been decorated. Tall residential buildings adjoin the main edifice on the east and west with 5,754 rooms for students and graduates, and 184 flats for the teaching staff.

On the south-western side the Physics and Chemistry departments buildings are ranged alongside the main edifice, and next to them are the premises of the Biology and Soil Department. Before the back entrance of the main edifice is a green parterre with a fountain and a bronze statue of Lomonosov, by Tomsky.

The main 32-storey edifice is occupied by the Rectory, the Geological and Geographical departments, the auditoriums of the Mechanico-Mathematical Department and the general chairs, an assembly hall with a seating capacity of 1,500 and several museums. In the centre of the building, occupying eleven storeys, is the depository of the University library of more than a million volumes. There are 33 reading-rooms. The University Club and gymnasiums are also located in the main edifice, comprising more than 22,000 different premises.

Let us enter the main edifice.

Beyond the columns of the portico are three entrances—three huge oak doors finished in bronze. Pass through one of them into the vestibule—a circular hall with a flat canopy. Its walls are finished in marble of bright, delicate hues, and the flooring is of polished coloured granite.

From the vestibule, through the cloak-room, you come to the lifts. The walls here are finished in red and white "Salieti" (Caucasus) and "Koelga" (Urals) marble. Gala stairways lead to the lobby of the assembly hall. At the foot of the stairs stand two-metre statues of Mendeleyev, Pavlov, Michurin and Zhukovsky. Brief passages lead from the lobby into the assembly hall. There is nothing superfluous or bizarre in the appointments. Chandeliers, at once magnificent and austere, are suspended from the ornamented ceiling. The shape of the hall is rectangular. Twenty-six white marble columns with gilt heads support a raised gallery. The walls are draped in gold-hued brocade, and the wall at the back of the stage is adorned with an enormous mosaic, covering an area of

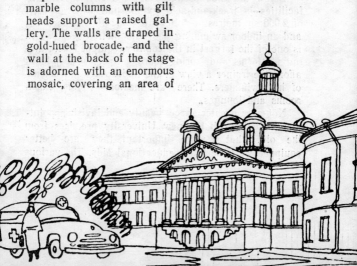

100 sq. metres. The mosaic is of red banners against a setting of gold.

A happy architectural scheme and the interior decorations seem to conceal the dimensions of the huge hall. Yet there is ample space in the parterre for 1,500 soft chairs. The galleries have room for another more than 600 seats. At present the University assembly hall is one of the most capacious auditoriums in the capital.

The main vestibule also communicates with the University Club. Here the visitor first enters a spacious lobby, which has a gallery for the orchestra and is often used as a ball-room. The Club auditorium is of modest size (seating capacity 800), but is superbly appointed. The upholstery is in reddish plush, which stands out against the white, faintly pink colouring of the walls. A huge chandelier of 200 luminescent bulbs provides "day-light" lighting. The stage equipment is of the latest, including diverse lighting devices and mechanical lifts to facilitate rapid changes of stage settings.

Below the Club premises are the physical culture facilities—a track-and-field gymnasium with an area of 2,000 sq. metres, a volleyball court (600sq. metres), and an indoor swimming pool four metres deep, which is one of the largest in the country, equipped with diving platforms and spring-boards. Special peep-holes afford the trainer a view of the underwater movements of his swimmers. There are medical rooms, cloak-rooms and lounges.

Not only greater space, beauty and lavish appointments distinguish the new University premises from the old. What is more important, they are better equipped with the latest educational aids. The various departments were built with an eye to their specific requirements: with huge glass cupolas of experimental hot-houses in the Biology and Soil Department, for instance, and installations to reproduce the Arctic and subtropical climates.

The Biology and Soil Department has its own botanical garden, which covers an area of 42 hectares. Thousands of specimens of the flora of the Soviet Union and other countries are represented there, and the garden has artificial "Alps," where diverse plants are cultivated. The tree nursery has a remarkable collection of trees and bushes, representing 500 species of the flora of many countries. An orchard has been laid, known as "Michurin Garden," where all the species developed by Michurin and his followers will soon bear fruit.

At present Moscow University has twelve departments: the physical, chemical, mechanico-mathematical, geological, geographical, philosophical, historical, philological, economic, and the departments of law, journalism, and biology and soil. The 210 chairs of these departments represent almost all branches of

modern science. The first five departments, and the Department of Biology and Soil, are in the new University premises, and the rest are in the old, in Mokhovaya Street. Moreover, the University has an Institute of Eastern Languages and an Institute of Post-Graduate Studies in the History of the C.P.S.U.

Moscow University has a body of about 18,000 students of 57 nationalities, and more than 5,000 correspondence students. Its teaching staff includes 89 Members and Corresponding Members of the U.S.S.R. Academy of Sciences, twenty Merited Scientists, more than 200 doctors and candidates of science, 400 professors and more than 500 docents.

At the time of its 200th anniversary in 1955, the Soviet Government decorated Moscow University, which already had the Order of Lenin, with the Order of the Red Banner in appreciation of its contribution to the development of science and culture, and the training of specialists.

The erection of the University buildings on the Lenin Hills marked the inception of a new district in Moscow's south-west. High-gear construction of dwellings and public buildings has been in progress there since 1952. The construction site stretches along Kaluga Highway and in length equals all of Gorky Street. In 1956 the first blocks of the development project, totalling 180,000 sq. metres of floor space, were completed. Towards the close of the Sixth Five-Year Plan period (1960) the south-western district will have 2,200,000 sq. metres of housing, 50 schools, and kindergartens and crèches for 20,000 children, stadiums, swimming pools, four department stores, seven cinemas and many other facilities. More than half of the new district will be occupied by parks, gardens, and boulevards, which will merge with the woodland of the Lenin Hills and with the University site.

The largest motion picture studio in the Soviet Union—*Mosfilm*—is located on the Lenin Hills. But it has become too small for the substantially increased production needs, and new facilities—the Bolshoi Mosfilm, which will put out several dozen full-length colour films annually—are now under construction in the south-western district.

* * *

On our way back from the Lenin Hills down Bolshaya Kaluzhskaya Street, we glimpse the *Donskoi Monastery* building at the end of Donskoi Lane on the right. The monastery building is an architectural and historical landmark of old Moscow. It stands on the site of a battle

fought in 1591 between Muscovy men-at-arms and the hordes of Kazy-Girei, the Khan of Crimea. The massive stone enclosure is built in the style of Moscow baroque—attractive and colourful, with lavishly ornamented walls and towers. At present, the monastery building is the site of the Architectural Museum. Models, drafts, pictures and photographs depict the work of many famous Russian architects.

Along Bolshaya Kaluzhskaya Street, past Oktyabrskaya (Kaluzhskaya) Square, we come to *Bolshaya Yakimanka Street*. A brightly-coloured house (No. 43) leaps to the eye—an effort in the late 19th century to revive old Russian architectural forms. On the opposite side of the street is a splendid example of early 18th-century architecture—the *Church of Ivan the Warrior*, built in 1713 at the behest of Peter I.[1]

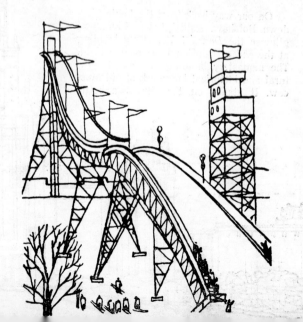

The *State Museum of Literature*, a unique institution located in house No. 38, possesses a substantial archive of manuscripts and a fine collection of rare books autographed by their authors.

From Yakimanka, along Kadashevskaya Embankment, we come to the *Tretyakov Gallery*, located in Lavrushinsky Lane. The gallery is, so to speak, a treasure-trove of Russian national art. It dates from the eighteen fifties, when a prominent Moscow connoisseur, patron of the arts, and industrialist, Pavel Tretyakov, started his collection of distinguished Russian paintings. Tretyakov regarded it a public duty to found a national picture gallery.

This collection of paintings, accumulated in thirty years, was supplemented by a collection of Russian 19th-century sculptures, which he inherited from his brother Sergei. In 1892 Tretyakov bequeathed his treasure to the City of Moscow. That, in effect, was when the Moscow Tretyakov Gallery came into being. At the time of its nationalization in 1918 the gallery had a little over 4,000 exhibits. Since then the collection has increased more than tenfold, totalling up to 50,000 works.

The Tretyakov Gallery affords material for a study of Russian art from the 11th century on. Among its exhibits are rare specimens—the glory and pride of Russian national art, such as the canvases by Perov, Aivazovsky, Shishkin, Vasnetsov, Kramskoi, Repin, Surikov, Levitan, Serov and many other distinguished Russian artists. In 1927 the Tretyakov Gallery founded a department of Soviet painting, sculpture and graphic art, which embraces the best works by Andreyev, Brodsky, Grekov, Ioganson, A. Gerasimov,

S. Gerasimov, Mukhina, Yefanov, Plastov, Bubnov, Serov and others.

The functions of the Tretyakov Gallery as a Soviet art institution differ greatly from those it had as a private collection, albeit one open to the public. It is no longer a mere depository of the best paintings, sculptures and works of graphic art. It propagates the arts, and conducts research. Exhibitions are staged periodically of works not usually on display. Tours of the gallery are organized, and public lectures are held about the works of individual painters. Many other fixtures organized by the Gallery are designed to acquaint the public with the treasures of Russian art.

The Gallery has its own restoration workshops, a library of works on Russian art, a scientific archive, and a file of about 100,000 negatives and photographs of paintings, sculptures and works of the graphic arts.

The Tretyakov Gallery is widely known at home and abroad. Up to 1,000,000 persons visit it annually.

From the Gallery we make our way back to the Yakimanka, and turn into *Bolotnaya Square*, which lies between Maly Kamenny Bridge over the drainage canal, and *Bolshoi Kamenny Bridge* over the Moskva. The drainage canal is an old bed of the Moskva, cleared, deepened and used as a canal to drain excess waters during floods, which were quite frequent in Moscow before the river banks were raised and reinforced. During the spring floods the entire area between the river and its old bed (the drainage canal) was usually inundated, and became a regular swamp. It is from this that the square derives its name, *Bolotnaya* being the Russian for swampy. By an ukase of Catherine II Yemelyan Pugachov,[40] the leader of a popular peasant uprising against the landlords, was executed in Bolotnaya Square in 1775.

During the construction of the present-day Bolshoi Kamenny Bridge (1938), Bolotnaya Square was remodelled. Old shops and stalls were torn down, and a pleasure garden with a fountain was laid out in 1952.

Opposite the garden, occupying the entire length of the short Serafimovich Street, towers a massive dwelling-house, by Iofan, erected in 1930. Serafimovich, author of one of the best works of Soviet fiction, *The Iron Flood,* resided and died in one of its flats. One of Moscow's largest picture houses, "Udarnik," is located in the building.

Behind the house, along Bersenevskaya Embankment,

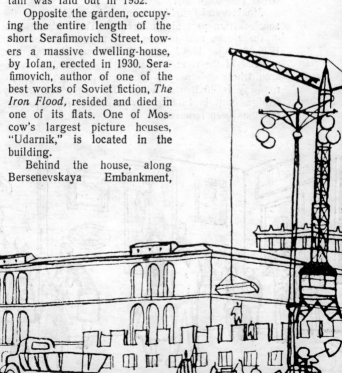

are the brick structures of the *Krasny Oktyabr Confectionery*, and beyond it, upon a promontory formed by the river and the canal, are the boat-houses of the *Rowing and Yachting Club*.

We turn from Bolotnaya Square into *Sofiiskaya Embankment*, which commands a splendid view of the Kremlin. The Grand Kremlin Palace is plainly visible, with Oruzheinaya Palata on its left, Blagoveshchensky Cathedral, Granovitaya Palata and Arkhangelsky Cathedral on the right, and Uspensky Cathedral in the background. The panorama is crowned by a view of the Bell-Tower of Ivan the Great (see page 38).

Moskvoretsky Bridge commands a view of the south-eastern part of the Kremlin. The bridge is one of the eleven new bridges over the Moskva built in 1936-38 under the Moscow Reconstruction Plan. The expanse of the river is spanned by a prettily curving arch, whose ends rest upon massive granite pylons. Its roadway is 40 metres wide. The old Moskvoretsky Bridge, built in 1871 somewhat east of the present one, has been removed.

On the left bank, right of the bridge, lies an ancient quarter of Moscow known as *Zaryadye*, formerly populated chiefly by petty artisans. At present it is the construction site of what is to be Moscow's largest hotel. The projected hotel will have 2,700 suites with accommodations for 4,500, while Moskva Hotel has 492 suites.

The set of hotel buildings in Zaryadye will include a theatre with a seating capacity of 3,000. In size it will greatly exceed the auditorium of the Bolshoi Theatre. The two-hall cinemascope theatre in one of the hotel buildings will simultaneously accommodate 1,600. The project will cover an area of 10.6 hectares.

SMOLENSKAYA SQUARE—MOZHAISK
HIGHWAY—FILI

The old road to Smolensk and the western frontier of Muscovy led from the Kremlin's Troitskiye Gate along present-day Kalinin Street and the Arbat. From Smolenskaya Square (in Sadovoye Circle) it descended to *Borodinsky Bridge* spanning the Moskva. The bridge was built in 1912 and bears the name of the battle fought against Napoleon's army near the village of Borodino. In 1950 the bridge was reconstructed. The width of its roadway was doubled to 28 metres, and the total width of the bridge was extended to 42 metres.

On its right construction work is being completed on *Novo-Arbatsky Bridge*, which will link the newly laid Novo-Dorogomilovskaya thoroughfare with the centre of the city and accommodate some of the heavy traffic now crossing Borodinsky Bridge. Novo-Arbatsky Bridge will be the biggest in Moscow. Its length will be 500 metres, and its width over 43. Two-tiered garages are being built under the overland spans of the bridge on both banks. Beyond Borodinsky Bridge, along *Dorogomilovskaya Street*, is a stretch of recently built houses. On the left sprawls the wide square facing *Kiev Railway Station*. In the centre of the square, amidst the flower-beds, the foundation has been laid of a monument to commemorate the 300th anniversary of the reunion of the Ukraine and Russia. The Kiev Station, by Rerberg, was built in 1917.

After the Revolution Dorogomilovskaya Street has changed its appearance. It is no longer on the outskirts of the city, and has become, along with Mozhaisk Highway, one of the city's central arteries. Kievskaya Metro Station was completed late in 1936, and in 1954 a second station, Kievskaya-Koltsevaya, was erected there.

The *Ukraina Hotel*, the largest hotel in the country, was built in 1957 in the vicinity of the railway terminal on Dorogomilovskaya Embankment some hundred metres from the river bank opposite the bridge construction site. The hotel comprises 1,026 suites accommodating 1,500 persons.

Beyond Dorogomilovskaya Zastava begins *Mozhaisk Highway*. If Dorogomilovo, which we have just described, was a typical outskirt of the large capitalist city in the past, its dingy workingmen's hovels nestling round a railway terminal built virtually outside the city itself, even less could be said of the one-time settlement nestling round Mozhaisk Highway—the

7*

most desolate and neglected section of the Dorogo-milovo outskirt. The settlement was not even within city limits, and was administered by the Moscow *uyezd* administration.

In Soviet time Moscow's former outskirts were radically reconstructed. They have changed beyond recognition. New enterprises, streets, squares, dwelling-houses, theatres, shops, bath-houses and hospitals have been built; the former outskirts now have trolley-bus, bus and Metro communications with the centre of the city.

The reconstruction of Mozhaisk Highway is vivid, convincing testimony of the triumph scored by Soviet builders over the usual antithesis of a city's centre and outskirts. Road-building began in 1937. Since then many comfortable multi-storey buildings went up in place of the countless little wooden hovels. The houses built in the late thirties bear the stamp of monotonous severity, but in later years architectural forms became more expressive and varied.

The reconstruction of Dorogomilovo continues. An ensemble of dwelling-houses is still to go up at the entrance to the city on Mozhaisk Highway. Novo-Dorogomilovskaya Street is under construction, and will end on the Moskva bank, merging with the new Novo-Arbatskaya thoroughfare, running parallel to the Arbat on the other side of the river.

The wide Mozhaisk Highway joins the 694-kilo-metre (430-mile) Moscow-Minsk autostrada.

On the city outskirt, on the right of the highway, sprawls the important industrial district of Fili. Near-by, at the far end of a small garden, is the so-called *"Kutuzov Hut"*—a spot associated in all Russian history books with the Patriotic War of 1812. The peasant hut was the scene of the famous war council called by M. I. Kutuzov[41] after the Battle of Borodino 120 kilometres (75 miles) from Moscow. At the council Kutuzov announced his decision to give up Moscow with-out a shot, well aware of the persistent need to preserve his army and prepare a counter-offensive. "The loss of Moscow does not mean the loss of Russia," he said, and ordered the retreat. History has justified his bold step and proved his military genius. The hut in which the war council took place, burnt down in 1869, and was subsequently restored in its original shape. At present it is a branch of the Borodino Museum of War His-tory. The display reconstructs the setting of the war council, and includes certain authentic articles, weap-ons and accoutrements, documents and maps.

The Fili settlement boasts yet another landmark—the *Church of the Intercession of the Holy Virgin*, built in 1693 for Lev Naryshkin, the uncle of Peter I.[1] The architecture and lavish adornments of the Fili church were so distinctive and fine, that they gave cause to speak of a Naryshkin style in Moscow's contemporary architecture

MANÈGE SQUARE—MOKHOVAYA ST.—KROPOT-
KIN ST.—LUZHNIKI (CENTRAL STADIUM)

Beyond Manège Square, on the corner of Kalinin and Mokhovaya streets, is the majestic edifice of the *Lenin Library*, the biggest public library in the Soviet Union. Not only has it up to 19,000,000 different books, journals, newspaper files, plans and maps, but an extensive collective of valuable manuscripts and archive materials. The library has publications in all the languages spoken in the U.S.S.R. and most of the countries of the world. Nearly 2,000 books and journals and over 3,000 newspapers from all ends of the world come to the library every day. Priceless specimens of Russian and world culture are preserved in special depositories. The library's department of manuscripts, for instance, has in its care 370 archives of writers, artists, public figures and statesmen, and about 30,000 manuscripts. The department of rare books has remarkable examples of the art of printing—books printed on parchment, silk and the thinnest of cork tissue.

The Lenin Library holds first place in the world for its number of readers, and books issued. It accommodates 2,000 visitors at a time, and annually issues up to 10,000,000 various publications to the reading-rooms.

For greater convenience the Lenin Library has both general and specialized halls, such as the halls of technical literature, medical and biological literature, historical and philological literature, a department of manuals and reference books, etc. The Lenin Library does not serve Moscow alone. It lends books to libraries in other towns and cities of the Soviet Union.

The library conducts extensive scientific and bibliographic research. Any enterprise, research institution, ministry, or individual, may obtain comprehensive bibliographic information on any subject, or problem desired.

The business of preserving books dozens and hundreds of years old is not simple. The library has a special department of hygiene and restoration. The latter, in its turn, has three laboratories: the entomologic, mycologic and chemical. The department and its laboratories are called upon to safeguard the books from "ailments," to "treat" fungus-infested volumes, eliminate mechanical damage, reinforce old pages, and control storage conditions. The most valuable and rare old books and manuscripts are mi-

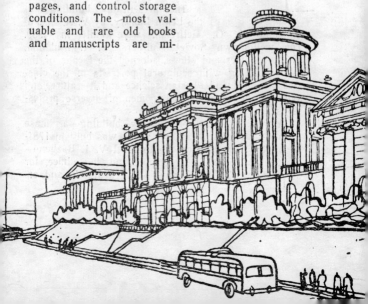

crofilmed. At present the library has accumulated more than 80,000 such microfilms, reproducing ancient volumes, manuscripts and rare printed matter.

The Lenin Library was founded in 1925, being a development of the library of the former Rumyantsev Museum, which was established in 1862. But that is merely a historical fact. The present-day Lenin Library has gone a long way from its predecessor, both for the number of volumes it contains, the number of its readers, and the scale of bibliographic work. Suffice it to say that prior to the Revolution the reading-rooms of the Rumyantsev Museum library had a seating capacity of only 400.

The present-day buildings of the Lenin Library, by V. A. Shchuko and V. G. Gelfreikh, were built in 1939. The well-known Soviet sculptors, V. I. Mukhina, M. G. Manizer and others, adorned the façade of the main building with sculptural portraits of the classics of world and Russian science and literature, and symbolic figures of working men of diverse professions.

Alongside is the old library building—a house formerly owned by Pashkov, which was built in 1784-86 by the famous Moscow architect V. I. Bazhenov. Simple and plain in its composition, the edifice, for all that, creates the impression of a stately and ornate structure, and was regarded as one of the old Moscow's most handsome buildings.

On the other side of the street, opposite the Metro station, is the *Kalinin[7] Museum*, devoted to the life and work of one of the oldest members of the Communist Party, an outstanding leader and statesman. Numerous documents, photographs, publications, and paintings, on display in the museum's nine halls, tell of Kalinin's part in the revolutionary movement, in the Great October Socialist Revolution, and of his contribution as Chairman of the All-Russian Central Executive Committee of the Soviets of Workers' and Peasants' Deputies during the Civil War and intervention, and later, as the permanent Chairman of the Presidium of the Supreme Soviet of the U.S.S.R.

A small street, the Volkhonka, is the continuation of Mokhovaya Street. The *Pushkin Fine Arts Museum* is in Volkhonka Street. The building, by R. I. Klein was completed in 1912. The Museum has on display more than 5,000 remarkable exhibits of antique culture and art going back to 4,000 B.C. The Ancient Egypt Hall contains a fine collection of authentic antiquities—papyruses, articles of worship, sarcophaguses, jars, etc. Giant statues of fantastic beings, and huge bas-reliefs, which are replicas, adorn the Asia Minor Hall, which has on display the antique arts of Babylon, Assyria, Persia and other countries.

Specimens of antique Greek and Roman art fill ten halls. The outstanding works of

the great sculptors of antiquity are here represented in originals and replicas. The halls of Hellenic art (III-I centuries B. C.) contain replicas of sculptured groups that adorned the town squares of ancient Greece. In the so-called Italian Yard are replicas of the most distinguished specimens of European sculpture of the 13th and 16th centuries.

The attention of visitors is drawn also to the picture gallery, which has on display many original paintings by West-European artists of the 13th-20th centuries. Among them are superb canvases by Italian, Spanish, Dutch, Flemish, English, German and French masters.

The Fine Arts Museum stages regular exhibitions of great masters of the past and present. Recently, for example, the Museum held exhibitions of canvases belonging to the Dresden Picture Gallery, the paintings and prints of Rembrandt, several of whose canvases were specially flown for the exhibition from Holland, and the paintings of Pablo Picasso, etc.

Behind the Museum, in Karl Marx and Friedrich

Engels Street, is a major research institution—the *Institute of Marxism-Leninism of the C.C., C.P.S.U.* The Institute collects the papers and manuscripts of the classics of Marxism-Leninism, prepares them for publication, and studies materials on the history of the Communist Party of the Soviet Union. Its library has the world's most comprehensive collection of books and periodicals relating to the history of Marxism and the international socialist and communist movement, totalling about 1,000,000 volumes, journals and newspaper files, including underground revolutionary publications

Volkhonka Street issues into Kropotkinskiye Gate Square. On the right is *Gogol Boulevard* with the surface vestibule of Kropotkinskaya Metro Station. In the end of the boulevard rises a monument of *Nikolai Gogol*,[15] the great author. The statue was erected in 1952 near house No. 7a, Suvorov Boulevard, behind Arbat Square, where Gogol spent the last years of his life.

Gogol Boulevard is the first of ten contiguous boulevards forming an incomplete circle from Kropotkinskiye Gate to Ustyinsky Bridge at the confluence of the Yauza and Moskva. The boulevards follow the former city wall, removed in the late eighties. The wall was built in 1593, and gate towers gave access into the city where it crossed the main streets and roads. There were ten such gates which gave their names to the squares: Kropotkinskiye, Petrovskiye, Nikitskiye, etc. The names have come down to our day, although the wall and its gates have long since been removed.

Ahead of us is *Kropotkin Street.* It bears the name of the eminent Russian geographer and traveller,

and one of the leading theorists of anarchism, Pyotr Kropotkin.

In the dim past a road from the Kremlin led across this location to Novodevichy Monastery, crossing open fields and meadows. After the big 1812 fire the area between Ostozhenka (now Metrostroyevskaya Street) and the Arbat became a residential quarter of the Moscow nobility, which fact left a pronounced stamp upon its quiet side-streets, lanes and cosy villas. A number of old-time mansions still stand, which are of interest to historians and architects. One of these is house No. 12, formerly a typical nobleman's residence with stables, service buildings, a garden and summer-houses. It was built in 1814 in the then fashionable "Empire" style. The composition is harmonious and buoyant, in spite of its dimensions.

House No. 11 is a wooden mansion in the "Empire" style, built in the early 19th century. Today it is occupied by the Lev Tolstoi Museum, founded on the day of the first anniversary of the great writer's death. Before the Revolution it was a modest exposition, collected by private individuals, relatives and admirers. In 1939 the Soviet Government decided to extend research of Tolstoi's writings and organize large-scale propagation of his work. All materials associated with the life and works of the writer were concentrated in the Tolstoi Museum, which is today one of the major literary museums in the country. It comprises an extensive department of the writer's manuscripts, a department of portrayals and memorials, a department of expositions and displays, a department of propagation, and a library. The Museum totals about a million sets of papers and objects relating to the life and work of Tolstoi.

It has, in all, more than 160,000 sheets of Tolstoi's autographs. The writer is known to have been highly exacting in his work. His manuscripts contain thousands of sheets of rough variants and corrections. The manuscript of *War and Peace*, for instance, contains about 5,000 sheets; *Anna Karenina*, 2,500 sheets; *Resurrection*, 7,000 sheets, etc. The rough variants of some of Tolstoi's essays total up to 14,000 sheets. All these autographs, from the first rough copies to the final ones, are preserved in the Museum's department of manuscripts. They show how scrupulously he worked on his books. The department also possesses some 10,000 letters Tolstoi wrote to diverse individuals. The total number of manuscripts in the writer's archives exceeds 500,000 sheets.

The department of portrayals and memorials is in possession of the writer's lifetime portraits and sculptures, including works by Repin, Kramskoi, Ghe, Nesterov, Trubetskoi, Aronson and others. The numerous sets of illustrations to the writer's works

by his contemporaries, and by Soviet artists, which are on display at the Museum, are of the greatest value. There is a special section of Tolstoi's portraits and of illustrations of his works reproduced on objects of applied art—porcelain, glassware, fabrics, etc.

Associates of the Museum conduct tours and advise visitors in all questions relating to the life and works of the writer. They also lecture on Tolstoi at clubs, schools and various institutions.

House No. 17 belonged to Denis Davidov, hero of the 1812 Patriotic War, partisan and poet (depicted in Tolstoi's *War and Peace* as Vaska Denisov). The magnificent colonnaded late 18th-century mansion next to it is the former possession of the Princes Dolgoruky. The adjoining building is occupied by the *U.S.S.R. Academy of Arts* and the *Institute of the History of the Arts*, a place of interesting art exhibitions.

Kropotkin Street issues into Zubovskaya Square. Beyond it begins the district of Devichye Field. At one time this was a distant and desolate outskirt, stretching from Zubovskaya Square to *Novodevichy Monastery*. Houses were built in this district in the latter half of the 19th century, and particularly after 1886, when a great many University clinics were erected there. Up to 1911, however, it remained a large, relatively open, space, the site of noisy popular celebrations with show-booths, swings, merry-go-rounds, itinerant circuses, pictures, etc. In our day Devichye Field is a splendid tree-shaded garden-square bounded on one side by Klinicheskaya Street, and on the other by Bolshaya Pirogovskaya Street.

Opposite the eastern side of the square rises the massive edifice of the *Frunze Military Academy*, by

L. V. Rudnev, graced by a bust of the leading Civil War general and subsequent People's Commissar of Military Affairs, M. V. Frunze.[10]

In the middle of the square is a statue of Lev Tolstoi[18] by People's Artist S. D. Merkulov. In the vicinity of the square, in Lev Tolstoi Street, is the home-museum of the great writer. Tolstoi bought the estate in the summer of 1882 and resided there until his removal to Yasnaya Polyana in 1901. In this period he wrote many of his works, and among them *Resurrection*, on which he laboured for ten years. Here he was visited by numerous friends and admirers, notably by Chaliapin, who sang to a small gathering of guests, and by Rimsky-Korsakov, Anton Rubinstein, Rakhmaninov and Skryabin, who played their music for him. Other visitors included Ostrovsky,[16] Chekhov,[24] Korolenko, Timiryazev,[35] Stanislavsky,[22] Nemirovich-Danchenko.[23] The artists Repin and Ghe painted their portraits of Tolstoi in his study, and, last but not least, here Tolstoi first met Gorky.[19]

After Tolstoi's death his wife sold the estate to the Moscow City Administration. In 1921 it was nationalized by decree of the Council of People's Commissars. It was visited by Lenin, who suggested that the historic and literary monument be restored. At present Tolstoi's home-museum has the appearance it had in the mid-nineties.

Klinicheskaya and Bolshaya Pirogovskaya streets are occupied by the numerous *Clinics of the Moscow Medical Institute and Hospital*, where extensive medical research and treatment are being conducted. A

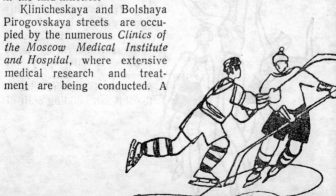

monument of Pirogov, the famous Russian medico and founder of military surgery, stands before the building of the Burdenko Surgical Clinic. It is inscribed with Pirogov's words: "Can anything be spiritually higher than the title of honorary citizen given by the Homeland to one of its sons not for brilliant military exploits, or material benefits, but for labour performed in behalf of enlightenment, science and social duty. In giving me the title of honorary citizen, the representatives of the City of Moscow have, as it were, realized the ambition of my youth, when I intended to dedicate my life exclusively to Moscow, the city of my birth and education." The monument was unveiled in 1897.

Bolshaya Pirogovskaya Street brings us to *Novodevichy Monastery*, a major historical and architectural Moscow landmark. It was founded in 1524 by Grand Duke Vasily III in commemoration of the liberation of Smolensk from Lithuanian rule. At the time it also served as a citadel, an outpost at the approaches to the city. It has powerful walls and towers, and stands upon an eminence on the Moskva bank, surrounded by large ponds. Architecturally the monastery, re-built in 1685-89, is an important relic of the Russian building craft of

the late 17th century. Only the brick walls, the five-domed Smolensky Cathedral, and the so-called chambers of Tsarina Irina (the "Godunovskiye" Chambers) still remain of the original 16th-century structure. A many-tiered bell-tower became the pivot and apex of the ensemble after the reconstruction. Its wooden carved ikonostases, the murals in the cathedrals, and certain ikons by the best masters of the day, are of great value.

In 1922 the Monastery was made a branch of the History Museum, and contains valuable exhibits relating to Russian history of the 16th and 17th centuries.

The cemetery of the Monastery is traditionally the burial-ground of many distinguished citizens, statesmen, writers, artists and actors. The tombs are adorned with monuments and gravestones by noted sculptors and architects.

Beyond Novodevichy Monastery, on an area of 176 hectares known as *Luzhniki*, bounded by a deep curve of the Moskva, opposite the Lenin Hills, sprawls *Lenin Central Stadium*, built in 1956. It comprises a set of sports grounds and structures. A lime-tree alley leads from the main entrance to the central sports arena, a

huge bowl with a football field. Its 72 rows of seats accommodate 103,000. The grandstands are covered with a sun-shade. A three-metre cornice girdling the outer vertical wall of the bowl diverts air streams from the stadium proper. Under the grandstands are 14 training gyms, judges' rooms, dressing rooms, medical quarters, a two-hall picture house, two restaurants, the Museum of Sport, and a radio and TV studios. The Palace of Sport, which is an indoor sports arena, is one of the most remarkable structures of the Central Stadium. It has a seating capacity of 15,000 and is one of the largest sports halls in Europe. But size is not all. The Palace of Sport has all the up-to-date sports facilities and is equally well adapted for ice hockey and figure skating, and for track and field events, tennis gymnastics and volleyball. The ceilings are sound-absorbing, eliminating the annoying hubbub usual in high-roofed auditoriums. The Palace of Sport is also adapted for concerts and public rallies, for which purpose it has a removable stage and armchairs.

South-east of the main entrance are the grandstands of the swimming pool, which meets all present-day requirements. Under the grandstands are train-

ing pools and a lounge. The vast grounds of the Central Stadium contain 8 football fields for training purposes, 18 volleyball, 18 basketball, and more than 20 tennis courts. Furthermore, there are four courts for the Russian national game of *gorodki*. There are also special grounds for other sports, such as gymnastics, acrobatics, fencing, weight-lifting, wrestling and boxing.

SVERDLOV SQUARE—KIROV ST.—KOMSOMOL-SKAYA SQUARE—SADOVAYA ST.—PERVAYA MESHCHANSKAYA ST.—YAROSLAVL HIGHWAY—U.S.S.R. AGRICULTURAL EXHIBITION —OSTANKINO

From Sverdlov Square there are direct routes to three of the city's railway terminals.

On the right side of *Teatralny Lane* are the remnants of the Kitai-Gorod wall with an archway leading to 25th October Street. On a green hillock is the *monument* to the pioneer of Russian book-printing, *Ivan Fyodorov*. The statue shows Fyodorov leaning against a printing-press, examining a freshly printed sheet. The monument was erected in 1909 on a site near the first Russian printing plant, the "Pechatny Dvor," built by Ivan the Terrible[3] in 1563, in which Fyodorov produced the first Russian printed book, *Apostol*. ("Pechatny Dvor" was located on the site of what is now the Institute of Archives at 15, 25th October Street).

Teatralny Lane issues into *Dzerzhinsky Square*. The square has always been a busy one, but its appearance has changed entirely. In the past it had a hydrant in the middle, to which housewives flocked with their pails for water. It had also a cab and carriage stand. Near Nikolskiye Gate, at the foot of the Kitai-Gorod wall, a brisk trade was carried on in cheap prints, books, patties, ribbons, tapes, pins, needles and thread.

At this point the Kitai-Gorod wall turned south, descending to the bank of the Moskva. Archways in the wall provided access to the three main Kitai-Gorod thoroughfares: Nikolskaya (25th October), Ilyinka, Kuibishev and Varvarka (Razin) streets. In 1934 the Kitai-Gorod wall was removed, giving way to a wide thoroughfare, contiguous with the streets mentioned above.

On the left side of Dzerzhinsky Square is the recently opened *Detsky Mir* (Child's World) Department Store. The volume of the department store building is about 300,000 cu. metres, and the shopping space alone covers 17,000 sq. metres. Eighteen escalators link the various floors. It employs more than 500 attendants. Farther on the left side of the square is the building of the Ministry of Internal Affairs, built by Shchusev in 1946.

Our ramble now takes us across Dzerzhinsky Square to Nogin Square, where, on the left, we glimpse the building of the *Polytechnical Museum*, founded in 1872 by a group of progressive Russian scientists, members of the Society of Natural Science, Anthropology and Ethnography. At present the Museum is in the charge of the Society for the Popularization of Political and Scientific Knowledge. Most of its exhibits illustrate Soviet engineering applied in the diverse branches of industry, electrification, mechanization and automation.

More than 20,000 exhibits are on

display in the 50 halls of the Museum, including machine tools, machines, devices, instruments, working models, dummies, collections of raw materials and finished products. There is the all-purpose high-speed screw-cutting lathe, for instance, and a working model of a fully automated blast furnace, an electron microscope magnifying objects to 100,000 times their size, a mock-up of a Kuibishev Hydroelectric Station turbine, and other objects of interest, including a number of unique exhibits relating to the history of Russian science and engineering.

The Museum conducts summary tours and special instructions, Sunday readings of "News in Science and Engineering," lectures on new engineering achievements and industrial progress, conferences and seminars on urgent problems of modern engineering, and many other fixtures to propagate modern engineering and progressive labour practices. The Museum library has a fine collection of books and journals in the Russian and foreign languages.

The Polytechnical Museum building also houses the Central Lecture Hall of the Society for the Popularization of Political and Scientific Knowledge, where daily lectures are held in all branches of science, engineering, literature and art.

Opposite the Polytechnical Museum is the *Museum of the History and Reconstruction of Moscow*, and farther on, between Kuibishev and Razin streets, are the premises of the *Central Committee and Moscow Regional and City Committees of the Communist Party of the Soviet Union*.

Near Razin Street, in little Nikitnikov Lane, is the Church of Our Lady of Georgia, a splendid example of early 17th-century architecture.

Dzerzhinsky Square is linked with Kirov Gate by Kirov Street (so named in tribute to the distinguished Communist Party functionary and Soviet statesman, Secretary of the Leningrad Regional Committee of the C.P.S.U., Sergei Mironovich Kirov[42]). In the past Kirov Street was a business centre of the industrial and commercial bourgeoisie.

In the beginning of the street, in house No. 7, is the Moscow *House of Scientific and Engineering Propaganda*, a meeting place of scientists, engineers and innovators. They discuss problems relating to the popularization of the latest achievements in machine and instrument production, points of their technology, and the progressive experience of leading enterprises and individual innovators. The House conducts excursions to plants and factories, offers consultations, and sponsors lectures by experts directly at plants.

Near Kirov Gate is the *Central Post Office*, built in 1911. Opposite the Post Office is an edifice by Bazhenov, built in the late 18th century. Before the

Revolution it was occupied by a school of painting, sculpture and architecture, which trained many prominent Russian artists. Such distinguished painters as Perov, Savrasov, Shishkin, Makovsky, Korovin and Levitan were associated with the school in the capacity of either students or teachers. V. V. Mayakovsky,[28] who besides being a poet was also a gifted artist, attended the school as well.

In Bolshevistsky Lane beyond Kirov Gate, is one of the most remarkable institutions of Soviet Moscow —the *City House of Pioneers.*

Along the relatively short stretch from Kirov Gate to Sadovoye Circle there is a curious mingling of architectural styles. House No. 33 is a modern structure built along simple, familiar lines. Alongside (No. 39) is a structure in the style of accomplished constructivism, erected after a design by the eminent French Architect Corbusier. Wedged between the two is a typical aristocratic mansion of the late 18th century (No. 37). In the vicinity, somewhat earlier than Corbusier, Architect Velikovsky also paid homage to the then fashionable constructivism by erecting another structure (Ministry of Trade) of glass and concrete devoid of all adornments (1925) at 47, Kirov Street. Next to it (No. 43), and opposite it (No. 42), are two more 18th-century mansions, the latter being by the famous Kazakov.[6]

Maly Kharitonyevsky Lane leads from Kirov Street to Bolshoi Kharitonyevsky Lane, in which Pushkin[25] spent his childhood. Opposite the ancient 17th-century stone mansion of the Princes Yusupov (House No. 21, now occupied by the *U.S.S.R. Academy of Agriculture*) was the famous Yusupov Garden—a popular resort of the Moscow nobility. The Pushkins resided in the vicinity.

Kirov Street terminates at Sadovoye Circle. We drive into *Lermontov Square* by Kirov Lane. The square bears the name of the eminent Russian poet, Mikhail Lermontov,[43] who was born in a house on the corner of the square and Kalanchovskaya Street. Today the site is occupied by the towering structure of the *Ministry of Railways*, which faces the square. The wings flanking the multi-storeyed central edifice are dwelling blocks with 11,000 sq. metres of floor space. The ground floors are occupied by a kindergarten and shops.

The central edifice contains 290 offices and a conference hall with a seating capacity of 300. The building has its own automatic telephone exchange, which provides its 10,000 subscribers with telephone and telegraph communications with any town and city in the U.S.S.R. It also has its own radio-relay station. The 24 storeys of the central edifice, plus the star-topped spire, rise 133 metres into the sky. The wings are eleven-storeyed. The edifice was completed in 1953.

Along Kalanchovskaya Street we descend to *Komsomolskaya Square*—the square of three railway stations. On the northern side of the square (to the left) is the old *Leningrad Station* of the Oktyabrskaya Railway, built in 1851, which connects Moscow and Leningrad. Beside it is *Yaroslavl Station*, built in 1906 in the manner of an ancient-Russian fairyland manor. It is the terminal of the longest, 9,000-kilometre

Moscow-Vladivostok railway artery, and of the direct Moscow-Peking passenger route. The flow of passenger traffic at Yaroslavl Station is considerable, totalling more than 200,000 passengers daily together with suburban traffic, and in summer, when numerous Muscovites move to the delightful summer resorts along Severnaya Railway, it is almost double that number.

Wedged between Leningrad and Yaroslavl stations is the surface vestibule of Komsomolskaya Metro Station—one of the first Metro stations to be built (1935), and of Komsomolskaya-Koltsevaya erected in 1952.

Kazan Railway Station occupies the entire southern (right) side of the square. Construction work on the terminal was begun on the eve of the First World War, but was completed only in 1926. Thus Kazan Station is the youngest in the capital. It was designed

by Academician A. V. Shchusev, who made harmonious use of various architectural motifs of ancient buildings in Kazan, the capital of the Tatar Autonomous Republic. The central tower of the station is reminiscent of one of the Kazan Kremlin towers—that of Suyumbeki (17th century), with which many Tatar legends are associated. Unlike its neighbouring terminals, the Kazan Station was built with an eye to the huge flow of passengers passing through it daily. It has spacious waiting rooms, a huge restaurant, a hotel for transit passengers, and several rooms for children. More than 100,000 passengers are accommodated at the station every day.

On the western side of the square, beyond the Okruzhnaya Railway, towers the 26-storey *Leningradskaya Hotel*, opened in 1954. The area of all the premises available in the hotel is 25,000 sq. metres comprising 350 single, double and three-room suites, halls, lobbies, two restaurants and a café. The 20th storey opens upon a flat roof commanding a fine view of Moscow. The interior is overly sumptuous.

There is a plan to reconstruct Komsomolskaya Square, envisaging a harmonious architectural ensemble. It is proposed to remove the railway bridge and lay a broad thoroughfare along Kalanchovskaya Street to Kursk Railway Station, with a Novo-Kirovsky Avenue branching off to Dzerzhinsky Square. The hotel will then be situated in an open site, and will serve to adorn the vast square. A large dwelling-house is proposed next to Yaroslavl Station, to complete the north-east side of the square. It will be an eight-storey building with a total floor space of 9,000 sq. metres. The ground floor is intended for shops, and the basement for garages.

We leave Komsomolskaya Square by Orlikov Lane for Sadovo-Spasskaya Street, and head for Kolkhoznaya Square. Here our attention is drawn to the building of the former alms-house, now occupied by the *Sklifosofsky First Aid Institute*. Among its most striking features is a double colonnade, whose centre curves outward toward the approaching sight-seer, adding greatly to its majestic appearance, further enhanced by the cupola crowning the edifice. The building is a first-class example of late 18th-century Russian architecture. It was designed by Architect Nazarov, assisted to some extent by one of the most gifted architects of his day, Giacomo Quarenghi, famous for the buildings he erected in Petersburg (Leningrad). The building was constructed for Nikolai Sheremetyev in commemoration of his wife, a serf-actress, whose curious story we shall tell in connection with the palace-museum in Ostankino.

We turn right from Kolkhoznaya Square into *Pervaya Meshchanskaya Street*. It has assumed its present-day appearance a mere fifteen years ago. The Meshchanskaya streets, of which there are four, took shape beyond the city wall. In the past they were inhabited by artisans and petty tradesmen. In the mid-18th century the eastern side of the Meshchanskaya settlement was nothing but open fields and vegetable patches. The wide-open spaces available in Pervaya Meshchan-

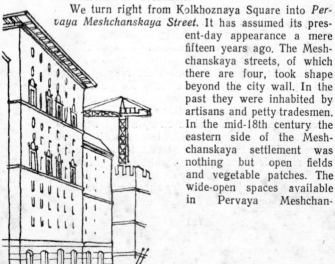

skaya Street caused Peter I[1] to transfer the Apothecary Garden of Medicinal Herbs from its former site at the foot of the Kremlin walls to that street. The garden is still there (28, Pervaya Meshchanskaya St.), but has, since 1805, become the *Botanical Gardens of Moscow University*. In the course of its 250 years the garden has developed from the "apothecary's patch" of Peter's Rus into a research and educational institution which in its time served as a scientific laboratory to a great many distinguished Russian botanists. It cannot be compared to the new Botanical Gardens of Moscow University on the Lenin Hills, but nonetheless occupies a worthy place among the educational institutions of the capital.

In the latter half of the last century a few rich manors rose along Pervaya Meshchanskaya. But they did little to change the general appearance of the placid, provincial street with its one- and two-storey cottages and flower-gardens.

Pervaya Meshchanskaya ends at *Riga Station* of the Kalinin Railway. This was formerly the city limit, the Krestovskaya Zastava, marked by two large water towers of the Mytishchi Water Works. Beyond it was Pyatnitskoye Cemetery (which exists to this day) and the city garbage dump.

Tremendous funds, and a truly gigantic labour effort were required to turn this former suburb into the present-day *Yaroslavl Highway*. The highway now begins with a handsome viaduct spanning the railway tracks. Thousands of cars, buses, trolley-buses and tram-cars move along the broad asphalt road. On both sides of it stretch new buildings—dwelling-houses, institutes and undertakings (the giant Printing Plant, for instance, in house No. 52).

Construction work continues in high gear even today.

A new street, Pervaya Yaroslavskaya, was opened last year. It has risen in an empty lot with all its large dwelling-houses, school and college buildings, and the guest-houses of the U.S.S.R. Agricultural Exhibition. The new thoroughfare leads to the right of the highway to Malenkovskaya Railway Station, where many new tall houses are under construction for the builders of the Metro. Thirteen houses with 110,000 sq. metres of floor space will go up in that locality before the end of the Sixth Five-Year Plan period.

Incidentally, the new thoroughfare passes hard by an ancient church, a relic of the 17th-century architecture. In the day of Yury Dolgoruky,[2] the founder of Moscow, there was an old trade route to Rostov-Veliky, Suzdal and Yaroslavl in place of the present-day Yaroslavl Highway. In the mid-14th century, when the Troitse-Sergiyevsky Monastery (now in the town of Zagorsk) was founded 60 kilometres (37 miles) outside Moscow, the road became a lively thoroughfare. Thousands of pilgrims walked along it to the Monastery, and among them were boyars, princes, tsars and tsarinas. In one of the villages along the way Tsar Alexei Mikhailovich built a roadside palace, and the mistress of the village, Princess Trubetskaya, built the Church of Alexei in its vicinity. The village then became known as Alexeyevskoye, which name has come down to our time for that particular locality. The mid-17th century church has also been preserved. The unknown architect has adorned the shapely edifice with white architectural embellishments which stand out strikingly against the red of the brick walls. Attractively framed windows, the intricate designs on the cornice, and a two-tiered girdle of caps round the five-domed superstructure draws the eye, testifying to the excellent taste of its commoner-builders.

Yaroslavl Highway leads to the grounds of the *U.S.S.R. Agricultural and Industrial Exhibition*, whose well-known steel monument of "Worker and Collective-Farm Woman," by Mukhina, and the gold star crowning the 100-metre (330-feet) tip of the main pavilion, are visible from afar along the way to the Main Entrance.

The *Exhibition grounds* cover an area of 207 hectares (511 acres). The area under plants, of which a fourth are exhibits, is 101 hectares (250 acres). On the south the grounds border the Dzerzhinsky Recreation Park in Ostankino and on the north side, the Botanical Gardens of the Academy of Sciences. The Exhibition comprises 307 pavilions and structures with a total volume of 2,000,000 cubic metres (70 million cubic feet). There are 35 kilometres (22 miles) of asphalt and 30 kilometres of gravel roads and alleys, with a round-the-grounds trolley-bus route.

The chief purpose of the Exhibition is to display and propagate all that is best and progressive in the work of collective and state farms, machine and tractor stations, and individuals engaged in agriculture. The Exhibition is a school of progressive agricultural technique for hundreds of thousands of visiting collective farmers, state-farm workers and farm machinery operators.

Each Union Republic and the major agricultural districts of the various republics (such as the Northern Caucasus and the Volga area, for instance) have their own pavilions. A substantial part of the Exhibition grounds is occupied by special pavilions where cows and sheep are exhibited, pavilions of hotbeds and greenhouses, pavilions of horse-breeding, flower-raising and bee-keeping, etc.

In 1956 the Agricultural Exhibition was supplemented by the *U.S.S.R. Industrial Exhibition*, whose purpose it is to illustrate the achievements of Soviet industry, engineering and science.

Its twenty pavilions and open-air displays exhibit machines and machine tools, instruments, models and

mock-ups. Many exhibits are shown in operation. General attention is drawn to the display of atomic devices applied in medicine and in the national economy, and to an operating atomic reactor.

There are several restaurants, cafés, shops, two cinema houses and an open-air stage. In the neighbourhood is a number of guest-houses for out-of-town excursionists visiting the Exhibition.

The Exhibition grounds have several entrances. By the gate issuing into Dzerzhinsky Recreation Park we come to the famous *Ostankino Palace-Museum*. From the eighteen forties to the Revolution of 1917 it was the suburban estate of one of Russia's wealthiest families, the descendants of Count Pyotr Sheremetyev, field-marshal and companion of Peter I. The Ostankino estate covered an area of more than 1,000 hectares (2,450 acres), half of which was woodland, whose mighty oak-trees and cedars up to eight metres (25 feet) in circumference were an object of general wonder and admiration. The remnants of this once mighty forest have now become a state preserve, in which are located the *Dzerzhinsky*[8] *Recreation Park* and the *Main Botanical Gardens of the U.S.S.R. Academy of Sciences* (400 hectares, or 990 acres).

The Ostankino Palace is a work of art. The entire edifice, erected by serf labour, is of timber (late 18th century). Among the serfs were gifted architects, painters, carvers, sculptors and carpenters. The construction was supervised by a capable serf-architect, Pavel Argunov,[44] a man of excellent taste, who designed the palace.

The interior decorations are not merely lavish and magnificent. They are executed with artistic perfection. The delicately elegant carvings in wood, the vivid, colourfully picturesque ceilings, the sculptural embellishments, the tiled stoves, and the parquet floors, are all in superb taste. Take the parquet, for instance. Each hall has its own unexampled design of flooring, artfully composed from differently coloured wood species. The birch, pine, nut and oak in combination with rosewood, boxwood, mahogany and ebony yielded both geometrical and intricate flowerlike designs, which, as it were, cover the floor with an expensive carpet. And in the round hall, known as the Rotunda, the flooring is composed of eleven different precious species of wood with tin and mother-of-pearl incrustations.

The Palace halls are filled with valuable paintings and sculptures by the greatest Western masters of the 17th and 18th centuries, rare prints, cut-glass and porcelain. The biggest hall of the Palace was a theatre —the pride and glory of Ostankino.

Nikolai Sheremetyev, owner of the Palace, was an erudite connoisseur of music and an ardent lover of the stage. It was, in effect, for the sake of the theatre that he built his Ostankino palace. The theatre, of

course, was merely a source of home entertainment and vanity for the fabulously wealthy grandee. Only men of his own station could attend performances, and that only at the host's personal invitation. On occasion, up to 200 such guests gathered at Ostankino. The performances were lavishly appointed. Serf-actresses appeared on the stage wearing costly jewellery. Among his many thousands of serfs Sheremetyev, who had an exceptional eye for talent, picked the most gifted performers, forming a remarkable company of 200 actors, actresses, singers, musicians and dancers.

The gifted actress Praskovya Kovalyova-Zhemchugova was the pride of the company. Her acting had the quality of inspired sincerity and profound understanding, and her dramatic soprano was exquisitely pure and heartfelt. The fate of all Ostankino is closely associated with her own. Still a child, she was taken into the theatre company from the poor home of a serf-peasant ironsmith. Her extraordinary beauty, talent and good nature won the love of her master. A year before her death, in the prime of her beauty and talent, Kovalyova became the Countess Sheremetyeva.

With Kovalyova-Zhemchugova's retirement from the stage and Sheremetyev's subsequent removal to Petersburg, the famous Ostankino serf-theatre, which holds an honourable place in the history of the Russian stage, fell into disrepair.

THE METRO

The question of building an underground railway in Moscow was first raised before the Revolution. The City Duma discussed it repeatedly. But house-owners, operators of public conveyances and owners of real estate stubbornly opposed the venture. It went against their interests. After the Revolution these obstacles were eliminated. When the progress made by socialist building provided sufficient resources for an undertaking of such magnitude, the Central Committee of the C.P.S.U. and the Soviet Government adopted the decision to build the Metro.

The heaviest traffic was always in the north-eastern part of the city, in the vicinity of the three major terminals of railway routes to all ends of the country, and of numerous suburban routes as well. Naturally, that was where construction work began on the first section of the Metro, the line leading from Komsomolskaya Square, via the city's centre, to Gorky Recreation Park, with branches from Okhotny Ryad and Smolenskaya Square.

Thousands of Communists and Komsomol members were sent by their organizations to take part in the construction project. They served as that integrating element, which unified the efforts of the builders and won them undying renown. The first section of the Metro constituted 11.5 kilometres of double tracks. On May 15, 1955, the Moscow Metro was opened to the public, and construction work began on its second section from Smolenskaya Square to Kiev Station, from Revolution Square to Kursk Station, and from Sverdlov Square to Sokol Settlement (in Leningrad Highway).

The experience gained in previous construction and the progress made by industry in the interim provided the Metro builders with superior techniques and equipment, which speeded up their rate of progress. In December 1936 a new line crossed the Moskva over a specially erected 500-metre long bridge and reached Kiev Station by a shallow tunnel.

In March 1938, after completion of the Pokrovsky radius, direct traffic was established between the Kursk and Kiev railway stations. The opening of the Gorkovsky radius from Sverdlov Square to Sokol Settlement in September 1938 completed the second section of the Metro.

During the Great Patriotic War builders worked on the third section. Under war-time conditions they faced tremendous difficulties. Many proficient and experienced workers had been taken into the army. Stringent economizing of means and materials was a stark necessity. Innovators sought substitutes for materials and equipment in short supply. There was also the difficulty of twice laying tunnels under the Moskva River and the drainage canal. But the builders surmounted all these obstacles and the new lines—from Sverdlov Square to the Likhachov Motor Works and from Kursk Station to Izmailovo Recreation Park—were commissioned in 1943 and 1944 respectively.

In war-time 1944 construction work was launched on the fourth section—the Metro Circle. The Big Circle, as it is called, was put into operation in sections. Traffic was opened from Park Kulturi (Gorky Recreation Park) to Kursk Railway Station (about 7 kilometres) in January 1950, two years later from Kurskaya Station to Byelorusskaya Station (another 7 kilometres), and in another two years, in March 1954, the Byelorusskaya-Park Kulturi stretch completed the almost 20-kilometre Big Circle. The annular route traverses 18 city districts, links 7 of the city's 9 railway terminals and has stations communicating with all the other operating radial lines.

Today the Moscow Metro has three lines crossing the city diametrically, and one annular line. The total length of all operating lines is 65 kilometres. The names of most of the stations are derived from the districts in which they are located, helping the passenger to get his bearings.

The Sokolniki-Sportivnaya line traverses the city from north-east to south-west via the following stations: Sokolniki, Krasnoselskaya, Komsomolskaya, Krasniye Vorota, Kirovskaya, Dzerzhinskaya, Kaganovich Station, Biblioteka Imeni Lenina, Kropotkinskaya, Park Kulturi, Frunzenskaya, and Sportivnaya.

From east to west runs the Pervomaiskaya-Kievskaya line, via Izmailovskaya, Stalinskaya, Elektrozavodskaya, Baumanskaya, Kurskaya, Ploshchad Revolutsii, Arbatskaya, and Smolenskaya stations.

The Sokol-Avtozavodskaya line runs from northwest to south, via Aeroport, Dynamo (stadium), Byelorusskaya, Mayakovskaya, Ploshchad Sverdlova, Novokuznetskaya, and Paveletskaya stations.

The following stations are on the Big Circle: Park Kulturi-Koltsevaya, Kaluzhskaya, Serpukhovskaya, Paveletskaya, Taganskaya, Kurskaya-Koltsevaya, Komsomolskaya-Koltsevaya, Botanichesky Sad, Novoslobodskaya, Byelorusskaya-Koltsevaya, Krasnopresnenskaya, and Kievskaya-Koltsevaya.

The lengths of the various lines are from 11 to 20 kilometres (7 to 13 miles), and the time of travel from end to end 17 to 30 minutes.

Work is in progress on three more Metro lines. The first of these runs from the operating Park Kulturi Station. Two stations—Frunzenskaya and Sportivnaya (near the Central Stadium in Luzhniki)—were commissioned in May 1957, while two more—Leninskiye Gory and Universitetskaya—are still under construction. Once completed, this line will cross the entire city, from Sokolniki to the Lenin Hills.

Another line is being laid from the operating Botanichesky Sad Station to the Agricultural Exhibition. There will be four stations along this 5.5-kilometre (3-mile) stretch: Botanichesky Sad, Rizhskaya, Shcherbakovskaya, and Agricultural Exhibition. Passengers will be able to change from the new Botanichesky Sad platform to the Big Circle.

The third line will run from Kiev Station to Fili as a prolongation of the Staro-Arbatsky Metro radius. It will run overland, however, rising to the surface some distance after Kievskaya Station. Three surface stations, Rezervny Lane, Kutuzovskaya and Fili, will accomodate this four-kilometre section.

A Kalininsky radius from Taganskaya Square to "Novaya" Station of the Moscow-Ryazan Railway, is also being contemplated.

An average of 3,000,000 passengers make use of the various operating Metro lines every day. Peak passenger traffic is from 7 to 10 a.m. and 5 to 8 p.m. Within these six hours the Metro carries almost half of its daily passengers.

The builders encounter difficulties every step of their subterranean way. They must not, at any cost, interfere with the city's busy life as they go along, and shun all possible damage to the city's vast underground network of gas pipes, water conduits, telephone lines, sewers, etc. Natural obstacles keep arising in their way all the time, of which water is the most treacherous. They come upon soil which they cannot extract without first drying or freezing it.

The Moscow Metro is an outstanding feat of engineering. It provides rapid, punctual, uninterrupted and absolutely safe traffic. It has a superior air-conditioning system, which adjusts the temperature in the sub-surface stations to 20° C. in summer and 12-14° in winter.

Escalators lower and raise passengers to and from the deep stations (which are in the majority), at a rate of 0.7-0.8 metres per second. The trip from the surface underground takes one or two minutes, depending on the depth of the station. Escalator capacity is 10,000 passengers per hour.

Six- and eight-car trains ply the Metro routes at minimum intervals of 1.5-1.7 minutes. The capacity of each line, therefore, is 34-40 pairs of trains per hour. A Metro car has seats for 52 passengers and ample standing room for another 120. This brings the capacity total of passengers per line per hour to 55,000 in each direction.

Average velocity, which takes into account the stoppages at stations, is 35-38 kilometres (22-24 miles) per hour. Metro traffic safety is provided for in the tunnel designs. Trains travel in one-track tunnels, each direction having a tunnel of its own. The lines intersect each other at different levels, and there is no switching along the route. Automatic blocking provides dependable traffic control.

The Moscow Metro is of considerable interest as an architectural feat. Its spacious, flood-lit, and air-conditioned stations are magnificently decorated. Their construction is made to cope with the tremendous weight of the soil and surface structures above them with ease and perfect security. This sense of security and ease is amplified by the decorative finish of their vaults. The walls and columns, finished in polished marble, stained glass or glazed tiles, add to the sensation of airy space. The passenger is spared the oppressive "subway" feeling.

Extensive use has been made in the interior decorations of stations and vestibules of natural finishing materials available in the Soviet Union. There is Ural marble—the light grey "Ufalei" and white-pink "Koelga"; Georgian "Shrosha" marble—dark red with white veins; the yellow-pink Crimean "Biyuk-Yankoi" marble; Ukrainian labradorite, and red porphyry from Lake Onega. The polished marble surfaces are durable and easily cleaned and washed.

Every station is of distinctive design. Appointments follow a definite theme associated with a given date, place or event.

There is Ploshchad Sverdlova Station, for instance, whose decorations follow theatrical motifs, because the station lies in the immediate proximity of the city's major theatres. Its vaults are adorned with columns bearing porcelain bas-reliefs illustrating the arts of the peoples of the U.S.S.R. The white marble walls, cut-glass chandeliers in bronze settings and gilded porcelain, create a cheerful atmosphere.

The near-by Ploshchad Revolutsii Station is entirely different. Its lines are simple and distinct. Arches of dark red marble span the passages between the hall and the platforms. They rest upon black marble bases, which simultaneously serve as pedestals for bronze statues illustrating themes of revolution and socialist construction. All the eighty statues are by Manizer.

Kievskaya Station is different again. It adjoins the terminal of the railway leading to the sunny Ukraine. Two rows of stately marble-faced columns, ornaments on the ceiling, the mosaic of the marble flooring, the stucco moulding embellishing the capitals, and the walls finished in marble of different colours—all this lends the station a vivid, colourful, southern appearance.

Mayakovskaya Station is regarded as one of the finest. Architect Dushkin achieved interior decorations, both simple and impressive, through the use of stainless steel, ribbed strips of which are set in the dark marble of the arch pillars. The pillar bases are faced with dark pink rhodonite. The oval base of the ellipsoid cupola is stressed by the lighting, which illuminates 35 coloured mosaics.

The Metro stations built during the Great Patriotic War reflect the heroic war effort of the Soviet people in sculptures, murals and mosaics. Novokuznetskaya Station, for instance, is ornamented with stucco bas-reliefs of battle scenes and with medallions bearing portraits of celebrated Russian generals — Alexander Nevsky, Dmitry Donskoi, Kuzma Minin,[13] Dmitry Pozharsky,[14] Alexander Suvorov, and Mikhail Kutuzov.[41]

Paveletskaya Station has a mosaic portraying the military parade in the Red Square on November 7, 1941, which covers an area of 100 sq. metres. The portal of Izmailovskaya Station bears the inscription: "Glory to the Partisans." The same theme is evident in the architectural design of the entire station.

Even greater scope and beauty is evident in the architectural and decorative appointments of the stations and vestibules of the Big Circle. Wide use was made of mosaics, and stained glass is used there in its own right for the first time. Komsomolskaya-Koltsevaya Station, we daresay, is today the most festively adorned, and the largest of all the operating stations. Seventy-two octahedral pylons support the airy vault, which is richly adorned with artistic stucco moulding. The colour scheme is superb. Eight mosaics composed of a hundred thousand fragments of marble, granite, jasper and smalt adorn the ceiling of the station's central hall.

Wide use was also made of mosaics in the decorations of Byelorusskaya-Koltsevaya and Kievskaya-Koltsevaya stations. The architectural adornments of Byelorusskaya-Koltsevaya Station are devoted to the heroic struggle of the Byelorussian people against the fascist invaders, and to the peaceful labours of Soviet Byelorussia. The theme is expressed in mosaics, sculptures and decorative ornaments. Bowls of marble and cut-glass supplant ordinary chandeliers. The ceramic tiles of the flooring create the impression of a colourful carpet. Kievskaya-Koltsevaya Station was designed by Kiev architects. Here again mosaics, of which there are eighteen, serve as the chief adornment. They are composed of precious stone and smalt fragments, framed in intricate ornamental stucco moulding. The mosaics depict memorable events in the relations between the Ukrainian and Russian peoples, from the Pereyaslavskaya Rada of 1654 down to our day.

Novoslobodskaya Station stands out among the others for its stained-glass panels, used for the first time in decorating subway palaces. The vignettes draw upon ancient Russian embroideries and fabrics for the motifs of their ornaments. All 32 of them are by Riga artists.

* * *

We have come to the end of our brief journey. The author and the publishers hope that the guide-book has helped you to acquaint yourself with Moscow. All suggestions and remarks concerning the present guide-book will be gratefully accepted.

BEAR IN MIND THAT IN MOSCOW:

1. Vehicles and pedestrians *keep to the right*. Honking is prohibited. Roads with heavy traffic may be crossed only at specially designated places.

2. *INQUIRIES* of all kinds—about private addresses, addresses of organizations, museums, theatres, cinemas, parks, and about routes of local and inter-city transport facilities, etc.—may be made at Mosgor-spravka Inquiry Booths at railway and Metro stations (open from 8 a.m. to 11 p.m.) and in almost all major thoroughfares and squares (open from 10 a.m. to 6 p.m.).

Private addresses may also be obtained at the Address Bureau, Militia Administration, 3, Pushechnaya Street.

Inquiries concerning lost property: in the *Metro*, Lost Property Department, Komsomolskaya-Koltsevaya Station, Tel. 90-21-40, Ext. 10-85; in *trams* and *trolley-buses*, Lost

Property Department, 22, Raushskaya Embankment, Tel. 33-00-18, Ext. 1-39; in *buses* and *taxis*, Lost Property Department, 76, Bolshaya Gruzinskaya, Tel. 50-13-70.

Inquiries concerning lost documents should be made at the Lost Property Department, Militia Administration, 38, Petrovka, Bld. "A," daily from 10 a.m. to 5 p.m. (except Sundays), and at Mosgorspravka Inquiry Booths.

3. *IN EMERGENCIES* dial 03 for ambulance; 01 for fire brigade; 02 for the militia; 09 for Information. Traffic accidents are checked at the Inquiry Desk of the Militia, Tel. 50-57-76.

4. *TRANSPORT AND COMMUNICATIONS.* Inquiries concerning train arrivals and departures are made at Mosgorspravka Inquiry Booths or the information desk of the respective railway station:

Byelorussia Station—Tels. 51-80-00, or 51-81-00

Kazan Station — Tels. 90-20-55, or 66-92-64

Kiev Station — Tel. 41-63-04

Kursk Station—Tels. 97-05-20; 66-61-27, or 97-82-50

Leningrad Station—Tels. 62-95-90, or 90-20-82

Paveletsk Station—Tel. 31-42-37

Savyolovo Station—Tel. 51-70-79

Yaroslavl Station—Tels. 66-73-28, or 28-42-63

Riga Station—Tel. 66-02-42

The information and booking offices of the internal airways are at 1/3, Maly Cherkassky Lane, Tel. 23-46-45, and at the airports:

Vnukovo—Tel. 95-66-00
Bykovo—Tel. 95-30-46.

Tickets for international air lines are booked at the City Air Transport Agency, 2/4, Sverdlov Square, Metropole Hotel, Tel. 21-45-13.

The Central Station of Inter-City Automobile Passenger lines is at 10, Zhitnaya Street, Tels. 31-54-52, 31-51-52, and 31-42-71.

The *Central Post Office* is at 26a, Kirov Street; Information, Tel. 28-63-11.

The *Central Telegraph* is at 7, Gorky Street, Tels. 92-27-58 and 94-90-40. The International Call Office is at the same address. For inquiries dial 41-20-40.

When using a *public telephone* drop a 15-kopek coin into the slot before picking up the receiver.

5. *MONEY*. The following bills are in circulation in the U.S.S.R.: 1-ruble paper bills (light yellow); 3-ruble bills (green); 5-ruble bills (light blue); 10-ruble bills (pink-blue) with a portrait of Lenin; 25-ruble bills (dark blue) with a portrait of Lenin; 50-ruble bills (greenish) with an oval portrait of Lenin on a dark background; and 100-ruble bills (light grey) with an oval portrait of Lenin on a dark background and a view of the Kremlin on the back. The 100- and

50-ruble bills have a watermark portrait of Lenin along the side.

Copper coins are of 1-, 2-, 3-, and 5-kopek denominations, and nickel coins of 10-, 15- and 20-kopek denominations.

A ruble is equivalent to 100 kopeks.

6. *MOSCOW TIME.* When it is noon in Moscow it is 11 a.m. in Sophia and Bucharest; 10 a.m. in Warsaw, Budapest and Prague; 9 a.m. in Paris and London; 1 p.m. in Gorky; 2 p.m. in Sverdlovsk and Ashkhabad; 3 p.m. in Omsk and Tashkent; and 6 p.m. in Vladivostok.

For accurate Moscow time dial 100.

7. *CHURCHES AND MEETING-HOUSES.*

ORTHODOX CHURCHES. Liturgy begins at 10 a.m. and the evening service at 6 p.m.

The major Russian Orthodox churches are:

Patriarchal Cathedral of the Manifestation of Christ, 15, Spartakovskaya Street;

Church of the Resurrection, 51, Rusakovskoye Highway;

Church of the Lamenters, 40, Bolshaya Ordynka;

Church of Ivan the Warrior, 46, Yakimanka;

Church of St. Nicholas, 1/2, Teply Lane;

Church of St. Pimen, 3, Novovorotnikovsky Lane;

The Troitse-Sergiyevsky Monastery in the town of Zagorsk (60 kilometres out of Moscow from Yaroslavl Station). Aside from ancient monastery cathedrals

where divine services are held, this is also the site of the Ecclesiastical Academy and Ecclesiastical Seminary of the Russian Orthodox Church.

The Holy Synod and Moscow Patriarchy are in Kropotkin Street, 5, Chisty Lane.

Some of the churches and meeting-houses of other denominations are given below:

Roman Catholic Church, 12, Malaya Lubyanka, services daily except Mondays at 8.30 a.m., Sundays at 8.30 and 11.30 a.m. and 6 p. m., on the eve of holidays at 6 p.m.

Meeting-House of Evangelical Christians (Baptists), 3, Maly Vuzovsky Lane. Congregations are at 6 p.m. on Tuesdays, Thursdays and Saturdays, and at 10 a.m. and 6 p.m. on Sundays.

Meeting-House of Seventh-Day Adventists, 3, Maly Vuzovsky Lane, services on Wednesdays at 7 p.m. and on Saturdays at 10 a.m.

Moslem Mosque, 7, Vypolzov Lane. The namaz is recited five times daily; Fridays at 1 p.m.

Jewish Synagogue, 8, Bolshoi Spasoglinishchevsky Lane; daily services at 10 a.m., and evening prayers one hour before sundown.

Old-Believer Cathedral of Byelokrinitsa Concord, 29, Rogozhsky Settlement; daily services at 8 a.m.

Church of Priestless Concord, 17, Preobrazhensky Val, services on the eve of holidays and holidays at 8 a.m. and 4 p.m.

* * *

8. The widest selection of *souvenirs* is available at the GUM, Red Square (ground floor, second line, near the fountain), and at special souvenir stores at 4, Gorky Street, 13/15, Stoleshnikov Lane and 10, Petrovka Street.

Fitting souvenirs are painted wooden knick-knacks —boxes, vases, ladles, cups, salt-cellars and other objects of original Khokhloma gold-black-red limnery, an ancient Russian handicraft developed in Gorky Region;

papier-mâché caskets, cigarette-boxes and powder-cases (lacquered) ornamented in the ancient Russian style on a black background made at the villages of Palekh, Mstera and Fedoskino;

carved mammoth- and walrus-bone boxes, paper-knives, picture-frames, and miniature sculptures by Tyumen Region (Tobolsk) and Arkhangelsk Region (Kholmogory) bone carvers;

vivid painted primitive clay figurines known as "Vyatka toys" made in Kirov Region;

Gzhel ceramics;

ornamental iron castings made at the Kaslinsk Works in the Urals;

various wooden plates, vases, shelves, caskets, hangers and pencil-holders made by Abramtsevo-Kudrino handicraftsmen;

carved birch-bark boxes with a coloured inlaid background made in Vologda Region; lacquered cigarette-cases, boxes, ash-trays and other objects from burl-roots.

Ural anhydrite, quartz, jasper and amber brooches, earrings, cuff-links, cigarette-hold-

ers, desk-sets and rings, available at "Russkiye Samotsvety," 13, Stoleshnikov Lane.

9. As a rule, *shops* are open in the following hours: provision stores from 8 a.m. to 8 p.m. (lunch interval from 1 to 2 p.m.) including Sundays. Other shops are open from 11 a.m. to 8 p.m. (lunch interval from 3 to 4 p.m.) except Mondays; on Sundays shops have no lunch interval and close three hours earlier than usual.

Some provision stores are open to 11 p.m., such as the "Gastronoms" in Okhotny Ryad and 14, Gorky Street; "Armenia," 17, Gorky Street; "Gruzia," 27, Gorky Street; "Gastronom," 12, Dzerzhinsky Street (open to 10 p.m.); "Gastronom," 2/54, Smolenskaya Square, etc.

The major department stores are: GUM, Red Square (open daily except Thursdays from 8 a.m. to 8 p.m.), Mostorg Department Store, 2, Petrovka (open daily except Mondays from 8 a.m. to 8 p.m.). "Petrovsky Passazh" (open daily from 8 a.m. to 8 p.m.), etc.

Works of Soviet fine art (graphic art and paintings) are on sale in art salons at 11, Kuznetsky Most and 15, 46, and 48, Gorky Street.

The special book-store of literature published in the People's Democracies is at 15, Gorky Street.

The store of dictionaries, text-books and foreign literature is at 18, Kuznetsky Most.

* * *

10. *Restaurants* are open till 24 p.m. Among the best are "Prague" in Arbatskaya Square, "National" on the corner of Mokhovaya and Gorky streets, "Metropole" at 2/4, Sverdlov Square, "Moskva" at 2, Okhotny Ryad, "Sovietsky" at 44/2, Leningrad Highway, "Leningrad" at 19, Kalanchovskaya Street, "Savoy" at 6, Pushechnaya Street, and "Zolotoi Kolos" at the Agricultural Exhibition. These restaurants have an European cuisine.

There is also a number of restaurants with national cuisines, such as "Ararat" (4, Neglinnaya Street), Armenian cuisine and Armenian dry wines and cognacs; "Aragvi" (6, Gorky Street), Georgian cuisine—shashliks, kupaty, satsivi, Sulguni cheese, etc., renowned Georgian wines—tsinandali, mukuzani, tibiani, khvanch-kara, tvishi, etc.; "Baku" (24, Gorky Street), Azerbaijan cuisine; "Kiev" (32, Gorky Street), Ukrainian cuisine; "Uzbekistan" (29, Neglinnaya Street), Uzbek cuisine—shashliks à la Uzbek, manty, pilaf, etc.; "Peking" (2/18, Petrovskiye Linii), Chinese cuisine, Chinese brandy and wines.

The *Moscow Race Course* (Leningrad Highway, 25, Begovaya Street). The races feature Orel and Russian strains of trotters specially raised in the Soviet Union at state stud-farms and state stables, as well as special training stables of many collective farms.

The course is elliptical; 1,600 metres for trotters and 1,750 metres for ordinary races.

Admission charges to the grandstands are 3, 5 and 8 rubles. The 8-ruble seats are opposite the finish.

Pari-mutuel booking offices sell 10-ruble "win" and "double" tickets. From 3 to 10 horses compete in each race, with 80 to 120 horses competing in a day of racing. Trotters compete the year round. Ordinary races are staged only in summer. Races are held on Sundays, 1 p.m.; Wednesdays and Fridays, 6 p.m.; and Saturdays, 4 p.m.

MOSCOW SPORTS SEASONS

1 Track and Field	all year
2. Weight-Lifting	all year
3. Wrestling (Greco-Roman and free-style)	all year
4. Boxing	all year
5. Gymnastics (heavy and free)	all year
6. Swimming and Diving	June-September in outdoor and indoor pools; October-May in indoor pools only
7. Water-Polo	Ditto
8. Rowing and Canoeing	May-October
9. Yachting	May-October
10. Cycling	May-October
11. Fencing	all year
12. Horsemanship	May-October in the field and summer manège; November-March in manège

13. Basketball	May-September outdoors, October-April indoors
14. Volleyball	Ditto
15. Tennis	Ditto
16. Table-Tennis	all year
17. Football (soccer)	May-October (cup and league matches); winter matches in February-March
18. Ice-Hockey	December-March in outdoor and indoor skating-rinks; May-September in indoor rinks
19. Skiing (jumps, slalom, cross-country)	December-March
20. Skating	December-March
1) speed-skating 2) figure-skating	December-March outdoors and indoors; April-October indoors only
21. Gorodki (Russian national game)	all year

INDEX

[1] *Peter I*, the Great (1672-1725)—tsar, eminent statesman and general. Able, dynamic and forceful, he carried out important economic, administrative and cultural reforms. Pursued an active foreign policy.

Encouraged Russian commerce and industry. About 200 industrial enterprises—iron works, textile factories, shipbuilding wharves, and several canals—were built in Peter's reign, invigorating Russia's economy and paving the way for a substantial development of its productive forces. Peter's administrative reforms strengthened and centralized the state. Had a hand in launching the first Russian printed newspaper, the *Vedomosti*. Architecture flourished, particularly in the new capital, Petersburg (Leningrad).

For all that, Peter's reforms, which involved tremendous expenditures, caused great hardships to the peasantry.

Peter's endeavours and flaming personality attracted many writers and poets. Pushkin, for instance, portrayed him in his poems, *Poltava* and *The Bronze Horseman,* and Alexei Tolstoi in *Peter I,* an epic novel. Pp. 25, 35, 36, 62, 92, 101, 125

² *Dolgoruky,* Yury Vladimirovich (1090-1157) — Prince of Suzdal, son of Grand Duke Vladimir Monomakh of Kiev. Founder of Moscow. Yury was known as Dolgoruky, meaning long, or grasping, hands. Pp. 59, 126

³ *Ivan IV,* the Terrible (1530-1584) — first Russian tsar, outstanding statesman of the 16th century. Went about strengthening the Russian centralized state with unusual persistence and energy, displaying ruthless determination and an iron will in the face of the bitter and treacherous opposition of the boyars, who strove to preserve the reactionary political system of feudal disunity.

Ivan's foreign policy was geared to the same task of strengthening the state. His several wars with the Kazan Khanate, which made repeated devastating raids into Russia, culminated in complete victory of Russian arms and the taking of Kazan in 1552. Ivan's reign is marked by important economic and political reforms, and by a marked development of Russian culture. He promoted book-printing; many eminent literary, political and historical essays were written in his day, and many edifices went up, including the St. Basil's Cathedral.

Ivan's unique personality was extensively portrayed in historical essays, books of fiction and works of art. Repin's famous canvas, *Ivan the Terrible and His Son Ivan,* for instance, is on display at the Tretyakov Gallery in Moscow, and so is the remarkable statue of Ivan by Antokolsky. Pp. 36, 44, 116

⁴ *Godunov,* Boris Fyodorovich (1551-1605) — Russian boyar prominent in the political arena under Ivan IV.

After the latter's death Godunov virtually ruled Russia under Tsar Fyodor Ivanovich, the son of Ivan the Terrible.

In 1598 Fyodor died. Young Tsarevich Dmitry, his brother and sole successor, had suddenly died in 1591. In the official version Dmitry's sudden death was ascribed to an epileptic stroke, during which he was said to have fallen on a knife and caused himself fatal injuries. But a rumour spread that Godunov's agents had assassinated Dmitry to clear Godunov's way to the throne. A month after Fyodor's death Boris was elected tsar.

A shrewd and clever politician, the imperious and ambitious Godunov continued Ivan's policy of centralizing and strengthening the Russian state. His court gained considerable power, intensifyng the system of serf bondage. This caused dissatisfaction in the people and bitter resistance on the part of the feudal aristocracy, who resented the restriction of their boyar independence.

This created a favourable situation for foreign interference. A sham Tsarevich Dmitry came to the forefront in Poland, claiming to have escaped from Boris Godunov's assassins. Sham Dmitry marched against Moscow at the head of Polish mercenaries recruited with the help of Polish magnates, captured the capital with the help of boyar treachery, and installed himself on the Russian throne. Godunov had died some time previously.

Godunov's dramatic seven-year reign became the subject of Pushkin's drama, *Boris Godunov,* whose theme Musorgsky used for his opera of the same title. The opera enjoys unfailing success on the Bolshoi Theatre stage to this day. Pp. 36, 37, 39, 48

⁵ *Rublyov*, Andrei (about 1360-1430)—painter. His works represent the peak of his contemporary Moscow school of painting. Although Rublyov did not overstep the bounds of mediaeval ikonography, he achieved a great depth of feeling, a delicate lyricism, and an unusual perfection of form. His best work is the ikon *Trinity,* exhibited in the Tretyakov Gallery. Rublyov was a monk of the Moscow Andronikov Monastery, where he died and was buried. At present the monastery building has been converted into the Rublyov Art Museum. P. 37

⁶ *Kazakov,* Matvei (1738-1813)—gifted architect of the 18th-century Russian classical school. A master of antique architectural forms, he skilfully combined them with a marked national theme. The many palaces he built in the late 18th and early 19th centuries did much to determine Moscow's general appearance. The most distinctive buildings by Kazakov are the Senate Building (in the Moscow Kremlin), the Petrovsky Palace, the House of Trade-Unions, and the Golitsin Hospital. Pp. 39, 54, 57, 60, 78, 83, 120

⁷ *Kalinin*, Mikhail Ivanovich (1875-1946)—a leader of the Communist Party and Soviet state. A turner, Kalinin began his revolutionary activities as a member of the "League of Struggle for the Liberation of the Working Class" founded in Petersburg by V. I. Lenin in 1895. Kalinin devoted 50 years of his life to the struggle for socialism.

A tireless Party propagandist and leader, Kalinin won the love of the working people. He took an active part in the October Revolution. For 27 years running Kalinin headed the supreme legislative body of the Soviet state, being elected Chairman of the All-

Russian Central Executive Committee of Soviets of Workers' and Peasants' Deputies at Lenin's suggestion in 1919, and in 1922, after the establishment of the Union of Soviet Socialist Republics, Chairman of the Central Executive Committee of the U.S.S.R. and later of the Presidium of the Supreme Soviet of the U.S.S.R. (1938). In 1925 he was made member of the Politbureau.

A museum bearing his name was founded in Moscow to commemorate Kalinin's services to the people. Pp. 42, 105

[8] *Dzerzhinsky*, Felix Edmundovich (1877-1926) — a leader of the Communist Party and Soviet state. In 1896 became a professional revolutionary, one of the most active participants in the Polish and Russian revolutionary movement. In 1917 he was made member of the Central Committee and Chairman of the All-Russian Extraordinary Commission to combat the counter-revolution and sabotage. In 1921 he concurrently assumed the chairmanship of a committee for the betterment of children's living conditions. He was greatly instrumental in eliminating child destitution—a widespread aftermath of the Civil War and its attendant destruction. In 1924 Dzerzhinsky was appointed Chairman of the Supreme Council of National Economy. Pp. 42, 129

[9] *Sverdlov*, Yakov Mikhailovich (1885-1919)—a leader of the Communist Party and the Soviet state. In 1901 he became a professional revolutionary. Repeatedly arrested and exiled by the tsarist government. An organizer and leader of the Petrograd (Leningrad) armed uprising on October 26 (November 7), 1917. He was the first chairman of the supreme

Soviet legislative body—the All-Russian Central Executive Committee of Soviets of Workers' and Peasants' Deputies, and concurrently one of the secretaries of the Central Committee. Pp. 42, 48

[10] *Frunze,* Mikhail Vasilyevich (1885-1925)—political and military leader, founder and strategist of the Soviet Army. Born in Pishpek, renamed Frunze, the capital of the Kirghiz Soviet Socialist Republic. In 1904 he became a professional revolutionary.

Sentenced to death by a tsarist court for revolutionary activities. As a result of a mass protest by workers the sentence of death was commuted to a long prison term. Escaped from the convict camp and participated in the Moscow armed uprising of October and November 1917. Headed many major civil war operations (in Turkestan, the Urals and the Crimea). After the Civil War, a top-ranking general of the Red Army. Pp. 42, 111

[11] *Zhdanov,* Andrei Andreyevich (1896-1948)—a leader of the Communist Party and the Soviet state. In 1917 participated in the Great October Socialist Revolution in the Urals. For ten years he was secretary of the Gorky Territorial Party Committee. In 1930 made a member of the Central Committee, and in 1934, one of its secretaries. In 1934-44 Zhdanov headed the Leningrad Party Committee. Then returned to the Central Committee in Moscow. P. 42

[12] *Razin,* Stepan Timofeyevich (died 1671)—Don Cossack, leader of a major anti-feudal uprising of peasants and Cossacks in 1667-71, which involved a vast area in the Volga-Don basin. After the defeat

of the uprising Razin was captured by the tsarist government and executed in Red Square, Moscow. The memory of Razin still lives in many folk songs and legends. His life was portrayed in a novel by S. Zlobin, *Stepan Razin* (1951). P. 43

[13] *Minin*, Kuzma (died 1616)—a leader of the Russian people's movement against the Polish intervention in the early 17th century. Merchant and elected head of the Nizhny Novgorod *posad* (now the city of Gorky), he called the townsmen of his own and other Russian towns in 1611 to collect funds and establish a militia to oust the enemy. He marched at the head of the militia from Nizhny Novgorod to Moscow, and took part in the decisive battle (Aug. 24, 1612) under Prince Pozharsky, in which the Polish invaders were routed and expelled from Moscow. Pp. 45, 139

[14] *Pozharsky*, Dmitry Mikhailovich (1578?-1642?)—prince and military leader. Participated in the struggle against the Polish invaders since 1608, and was invited to Nizhny Novgorod to head Minin's militia in 1611. Pp. 45, 139

[15] *Gogol*, Nikolai Vasilyevich (1809-1852)—writer. Gogol's works are a mixture of impassioned realistic satire, a profound love of man, and lyrical beauty. Author of many novels, stories and plays. His best-known are: *Dead Souls, Taras Bulba, Evenings Near the Village of Dikanka, Mirgorod,* and the plays, *Inspector-General* and *Marriage.* Pp. 52, 107

[16] *Ostrovsky*, Alexander Nikolayevich (1823-1886)—playwright, realist. Born in Zamoskvorechye, a Moscow merchant quarter. Ostrovsky lays the bigoted,

savage morals of Russian merchants. The Maly Theatre, with which he was intimately associated, was
also known as Ostrovsky House. His plays, *The Storm,
Forest, A Lucrative Post, Dowerless, Guilty Without
Blame* and many others, run on the Soviet stage to
this day with unfailing success. Pp. 52, 53, 82, 111

[17] *Turgenev*, Ivan Sergeyevich (1818-1883)—writer.
Turgenev's early penchant for literature developed
under the marked influence of Pushkin, Gogol and
Lermontov. Turgenev authored such novels as
Rudin (1856), *A Nest of the Gentry* (1859), *On the
Eve* (1860), *Fathers and Sons* (1862), *Smoke* (1867),
Novelty (1877), which constitute a kind of spiritual
history of several generations. His deep-felt por-
trayals of landscapes have won Turgenev fame as a
bard of Russian nature. Turgenev has done much to
develop contacts between Russian and Western
literature. He spent most of his life in Europe,
where he had a brilliant circle of friends, including
George Sand, Prosper Mérimée, Gustave Flaubert,
Emile Zola, Guy de Maupassant, Alphonse Daudet.
P. 52

[18] *Tolstoi*, Lev Nikolayevich (1828-1910)—great Russian writer. Born at Yasnaya Polyana, a family estate near the city of Tula, where he spent most of
his life. Now the estate is a museum, a centre of attraction for numerous visitors. The great writer is
also buried at Yasnaya Polyana. Tolstoi is the leading exponent of critical realism in world literature
and a master of penetrating psychological analysis.
His greatest novels are *War and Peace, Anna Karenina* and *Resurrection.* Tolstoi was a prolific writer,
his complete works numbering 90 volumes. Pp. 52, 111

[19] *Gorky*, Maxim (pen-name of Alexei Maximovich Peshkov) (1868-1936)—writer, pioneer of Soviet literature, prominent essayist and literary critic. In his books Gorky depicted the finest traits of the Russian national character. Pp. 52, 68, 80, 111

[20] *Herzen*, Alexander Ivanovich (1812-1870)—revolutionary democrat, materialist philosopher, essayist and writer. Persecuted by the tsarist police, the free-thinking writer emigrated to Western Europe in 1847. In 1852 he settled in London, where he established a free Russian press. Published the *Polyarnaya Zvezda* (Polar Star), an almanac, and *Kolokol* (Bell), which exercised a marked influence on the development of the Russian revolutionary democratic movement. Died in Paris and was interred in Nice. Pp. 57, 85

[21] *Ogaryov*, Nikolai Platonovich (1813-1877)—revolutionary democrat, gifted poet and essayist, philosopher and musician. Herzen's friend and associate with whom he collaborated in establishing a free Russian press in London. P. 57

[22] *Stanislavsky* (Alexeyev), Konstantin Sergeyevich (1863-1938)—producer, actor, instructor of stage-craft, stage theorist, founder of a new stage system. In 1898 founded the Moscow Art Theatre in collaboration with Vladimir Ivanovich Nemirovich-Danchenko. Headed the theatre until his death. Pp. 59, 61, 66, 111

[23] *Nemirovich-Danchenko*, Vladimir Ivanovich (1858-1943)—producer, dramatist and writer. Founded the Moscow Art Theatre (1898) in collaboration with

Stanislavsky. Was in charge of its repertoire, and worked in the capacity of producer. After Stanislavsky's death (1938) took full charge of the theatre. Pp. 59, 111

24 *Chekhov*, Anton Pavlovich (1860-1904)—writer. Studied medicine at Moscow University. First began to write humorous stories and feuilletons for newspapers and magazines while still a University student. Developed into one of the most distinguished writers of the late 19th century, pioneer of Russian short-story writing, which he raised to a genuine art. Chekhov created the drama of moods, four of his best-known plays, *Sea-Gull, Uncle Vanya, Three Sisters* and *Cherry Orchard*, occupying a special place in Russian dramaturgy. They had a profound influence on the development of the theatre, particularly the Moscow Art Theatre. Pp. 61, 77, 111

25 *Pushkin*, Alexander Sergeyevich (1799-1837)—great Russian poet, founder of modern Russian literature, whose fine language set the standards of the Russian literary tongue. Pushkin wrote numerous poems, verses and prose—epigrams, lyrical poetry, romantic or epic poems, and heroic tragedies, short stories and historical novels. His best-known works are: *Yevgeny Onegin,* a novel in verse, *Boris Godunov,* a historical tragedy, *Ruslan and Lyudmila,* a poem, *The Gypsies, The Bronze Horseman, The Captain's Daughter,* a historical novel, *The Little Tragedies, The Miserly Knight, Mozart and Sallieri,* etc.

Pushkin's deeply realistic works had a marked effect on the further development of Russian literature. His poetry inspired numerous distinguished

Russian composers, who applied its themes in their romances, operas and ballets. Pp. 62, 63, 65, 69, 71, 120

26 *Griboyedov*, Alexander Sergeyevich (1795-1829) — dramatist, poet, and distinguished diplomat. His comedy in verse, *Wit Works Woe* (1824), is one cf the greatest Russian plays, a brilliant portrayal of his contemporary Russian aristocracy. Griboyedov died tragically in Persia, where he was Russia's plenipotentiary resident-minister. P. 65

27 *Zhukovsky*, Nikolai Yegorovich (1847-1921) — founder of modern hydroaeromechanics, "father of Russian aviation," researcher in aerodynamics, aviation, hydraulics, hydrodynamics, mathematics and astronomy. Founder of the Central Aero-Hydrodynamic Institute and the Air Force Academy (both institutions bearing his name), whose school of aerodynamicists now carries on his life's work. Zhukovsky was an honorary member of many foreign universities, including Oxford University. Pp. 72, 85

28 *Mayakovsky*, Vladimir Vladimirovich (1893-1930) — outstanding Soviet poet, brilliant innovator of poetical form, citizen-poet, fighter-poet who associated his entire life with the revolutionary cause. Mayakovsky was also a writer of fine lyrical poetry. Had a good deal of influence on the development of Soviet poetry. His best-known works are the poems *Lenin, Good,* and *About This,* and the plays, *Bug* and *Bath-House,* etc. Pp. 75, 120

29 *Chaikovsky*, Pyotr Ilyich (1840-1893) — composer who gave the world exquisite music in various forms — symphonies, operas, ballets, orchestral works,

piano, trios and plays, string quartets and sextets, romances, and several works for virtuoso recitals.

Chaikovsky's operas, *Queen of Spades, Yevgeny Onegin, Iolanta, Cherevichki (Vakula the Blacksmith), Mazepa,* and his ballets, *The Nutcracker, Swan Lake,* and *The Sleeping Beauty,* appear on the Soviet stage with unfailing success to this day.

Chaikovsky spent the last few years of his life in Klin (90 kilometres out of Moscow by the Oktyabrskaya Railway). His Klin home is now a memorial museum. A statue of the great composer was unveiled in 1954 in Herzen Street, Moscow, outside the Conservatoire bearing his name. Pp. 76, 78

[30] *Lomonosov,* Mikhail Vasilyevich (1711-1765)—encyclopaedist, materialist thinker, one of the founders of the modern natural sciences, and a poet who laid the foundations of the modern Russian literary tongue.

Born in Arkhangelsk Gubernia in the family of a *pomor* peasant, young Lomonosov walked to Moscow in the winter of 1730 to quench his acute thirst for knowledge. He joined the Moscow Slav-Greco-Latin Academy. On leaving the Academy he spent three years at Marburg University. In 1745 Lomonosov was made professor (academician) of chemistry of the Petersburg Academy of Sciences. Lomonosov devoted himself to the development of Russian science and culture, dealing with problems concerning almost all branches of his contemporary natural sciences, mining and metallurgy, philology, history and poetry. Made many scientific discoveries. Showed great concern for the spread of education in Russia

He was instrumental in the establishment of Moscow University in 1755. P. 85.

[31] *Lobachevsky*, Nikolai Ivanovich (1792-1856)—mathematician, founder of non-Euclidian geometry. In his capacity of Rector of Kazan University, Professor Lobachevsky founded a new geometrical system known as hyperbolic, or Lobachevskian, geometry, the turning-point in the development of 19th-century mathematical thought. P. 85

[32] *Chernyshevsky*, Nikolai Gavrilovich (1828-1889)—revolutionary democrat, economist, philosopher, historian, politician, literary critic and writer. Propagated the ideas of materialism, peasant revolution, hatred of serfdom, and love of knowledge, freedom and faith in a new world of justice. Spent 21 years of his life in prisons, labour camps and in exile. P. 85

[33] *Mendeleyev*, Dmitry Ivanovich (1834-1907)—the greatest chemist of the 19th century. Discovered the periodic law of elements (Mendeleyev's Periodic System), which forms the basis of the modern conception of substances. The periodic law, in its later development, revealed the objective regularity of the inorganic world, the mutual bonds between elements, propounded the idea of their tendency to transformation, and the principle of evolution in chemistry. Mendeleyev made a number of important discoveries in other branches of chemistry. He was a member of the London Royal Society, the academies at Rome, Paris, Berlin, etc., and honorary member of many scientific societies in Russia, Western Europe and America. P. 85

[34] *Popov*, Alexander Stepanovich (1859-1905)—scientist, inventor of the radio. Studied physics and mathematics at Petersburg University, which he graduated in 1882. In 1896 Popov demonstrated to the Russian Society of Physics and Chemistry the transmission of wireless signals over a distance of 250 metres—the world's first radiogramme. P. 85

[35] *Timiryazev*, Kliment Arkadyevich (1843-1929)—scientist, botanist, physiologist, gifted propagator of scientific knowledge. His research in the sphere of photosynthesis of plants is of utmost importance. He was honorary member of Glasgow, Cambridge and Geneva universities, a member of the London Royal Society, the Edinburgh and Manchester botanical societies, honorary member of many Russian universities and scientific bodies.

A convinced democrat, Timiryazev sided from the first with the Soviet system, and devoted himself whole-heartedly to public service. A monument to Timiryazev has been erected in the capital. The Moscow Agricultural Academy bears his name, and so does the entire district in which it is located. Pp. 85, 111

[36] *Michurin*, Ivan Vladimirovich (1855-1935)—naturalist, biologist-selector and geneticist, who proved in practice that man can direct the evolution of plants, i. e., alter the hereditary characteristics of organisms. Michurin developed about 300 new species of fruits and berries, highly popular throughout the Soviet Union. Michurin's experiments passed under the slogan: "We cannot wait for favours from nature; we must wrest them from her." The

city of Kozlov, Tambov Region, where Michurin spent his life, has been renamed Michurinsk. P. 85

37 *Pavlov*, Ivan Petrovich (1849-1936)—physiologist, founder of the materialist teaching on the higher nervous activity of men and animals. He laid the foundation of materialist psychology, and elaborated new principles of physiological research, which facilitate the study of a body's activity as an integral whole in interaction with its environment Pavlov was the first to show that all vital processes in men and animals are interconnected and interdependent, that they are in a constant state of activity and development, and that they are subject to objective laws. He was an honorary member of many Russian and foreign scientific societies, academies, universities, etc. In 1935 at the 15th International Congress of Physiologists he was given the title of "Dean of the physiological world." P. 85.

38 *Dokuchayev*, Vasily Vasilyevich (1846-1903)—naturalist, founder of the modern soil science. In tribute to the scientist the Soviet Government gave his name to gold medals and prizes conferred for outstanding research in the sphere of soil science. P. 85

39 *Chebyshev*, Pafnuty Lvovich (1821-1894)—mathematician. Made a number of important discoveries. Chebyshev and his followers laid the foundation of the modern theory of probability in its application to the national sciences. He was an honorary member of all the Russian universities and a corresponding member of many West-European scientific societies. P. 85

[40] *Pugachov*, Yemelyan (about 1742-1775)—Don Cossack, leader of a major anti-feudal uprising of peasants and Cossacks in the eighteen seventies in the Volga area and the Urals. Assumed the name of Tsar Peter III. Pugachov nurtured a plan of capturing Moscow and Petersburg and establishing a system much like that of Cossack self-administration. In August 1774 Pugachov's army suffered total defeat. He was taken prisoner, brought to Moscow, and executed in Bolotnaya Square.

Pugachov's life attracted the interest of many writers, particularly Pushkin, who portrayed the popular hero in his *Captain's Daughter* and the uncompleted *History of the Pugachov Mutiny*. In Soviet fiction Pugachov and his peasant uprising are depicted in Vyacheslav Shishkov's historical novel, *Yemelyan Pugachov*. P. 95

[41] *Kutuzov*, Mikhail Illarionovich (1745-1813)—field-marshal, one of the founders of progressive Russian warcraft. Educated at an artillery engineering school, he participated in the Russo-Turkish wars of the latter half of the 18th century. During Napoleon's invasion (1812) Kutuzov was appointed supreme commander of the Russian army and ousted Napoleon's troops from Russia. In 1942, during the Great Patriotic War, the Order of Kutuzov was instituted in the Soviet Army as one of the highest Soviet military decorations. Pp. 101, 139

[42] *Kirov* (Kostrikov), Sergei Mironovich (1886-1934) —a leader of the Communist Party, professional revolutionary since 1904 and an active participant in three Russian revolutions (1905, February 1917, and October 1917). From 1926 to the day of his death

Kirov headed the Leningrad Party Committee. The reconstruction and development of Leningrad's industries and of the agriculture of Leningrad Region were effected under his control. In 1934 Kirov was assassinated by counter-revolutionaries. P. 119

[43] *Lermontov*, Mikhail Yuryevich (1814-1841)—poet, major exponent of Russian revolutionary and romantic poetry, a citizen and rebel poet. Lermontov's insurgent ideas are particularly marked in the poem *Demon*, on which Lermontov worked for many years (from 1829). Its theme was used by Rubinstein in his opera of the same name, popular in the U.S.S.R. to this day. Lermontov is the author of numerous verses and poems. His major work in prose is the novel, *Hero of Our Time,* in which he displayed his mastery of psychological realism. He was exiled to the Caucasus for his mutinous verses and was killed in a duel secretly provoked by the tsarist gendarmerie. P. 121

[44] *Argunov*, Pavel Ivanovich (1768-1806)—one of the Argunovs, a family of gifted Russian artists, serfs of Count Sheremetyev. Pavel was a gifted self-educated architect, who learnt drawing and draftsmanship from his father. Sheremetyev's famous Ostankino palace and theatre was built under his supervision. P. 129

Printed in the Union of Soviet Socialist Republics

1

2

3

6

7

18

19

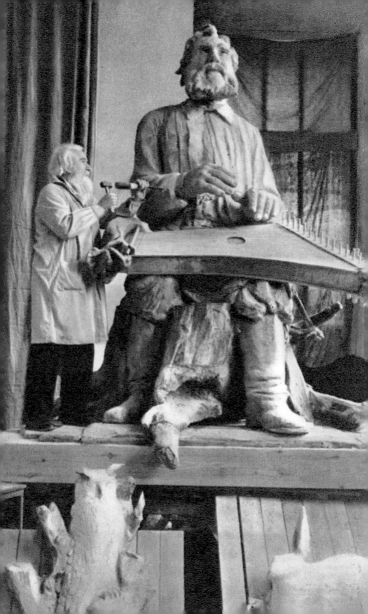

20

21

30

31

33

32

38

46

47